Graduate Job Search

Stephen Ling

CENTURY
BUSINESS

This edition first published in the United Kingdom by Century Ltd Random House, 20 Vauxhall Bridge Road, London SW1V 2SA

Random House Australia (Pty) Limited
20 Alfred Street, Milsons Point,
Sydney, New South Wales 2061, Australia

Random House New Zealand Limited
18 Poland Road, Glenfield
Auckland 10, New Zealand

Random House South Africa (Pty) Limited
Endulini, 5a Jubilee Road, Parktown 2193, South Africa

Random House UK Limited Reg. No. 954009

Papers used by Random House UK Limited are natural, recyclable products made from wood grown in sustainable forests. The manufacturing processes conform to the environmental regulations of the country of origin.

Companies, institutions and other organizations wishing to make bulk purchases of any business books published by Random House should contact their local bookstore or Random House direct: The Special Sales Director,
Random House, 20 Vauxhall Bridge Road, London SW1V 2SA
Tel: 0171 840 8470 Fax 0171 828 6681

Random House UK Limited Reg. No. 954009

ISBN 0 7126 7872 7

Typeset by Palimpsest Book Production Limited,
Polmont, Stirlingshire
Printed and bound in Great Britain by
Mackays of Chatham plc, Chatham, Kent

Contents

Introduction   1

PART 1: THE PLAN
Chapter 1   A Plan for a Job Search   5
Chapter 2   Reviewing Your Skills   18
Chapter 3   Personality   26
Chapter 4   Choosing Your Job   33
Chapter 5   Professional Help   38

PART 2: THE JOB APPLICATION
Chapter 6   Writing a CV   43
Chapter 7   Application Forms   55
Chapter 8   Advertisements   62
Chapter 9   Speculative Approaches   67
Chapter 10   The Milk Round   74

PART 3: THE INTERVIEW
Chapter 11   Interview Preparation   85
Chapter 12   Practice   104
Chapter 13   Questions and Answers   109
Chapter 14   Interview Surprises   120

Further Reading   132

Index   134

Introduction

This book is directed at all graduates. You may be about to graduate, recently graduated but not yet professionally employed, or you could be looking for a change of job after several years' experience.

We are witnessing an increase in the graduate population at a time when the supply of suitable jobs is stagnant. There is increasing competition for those jobs that provide relevant professional experience. Further, loyalty to employers is declining, while job insecurity is increasing. There are no longer jobs for life. Experienced graduates are more and more willing to move jobs to capitalise on their experience. They are increasingly having to look for jobs when redundant.

In my graduate career, I moved job four times in twenty years. I worked for major companies including Fisons, British Gas and ICI. I attended over fifty interviews, securing twelve job offers. Most recently I experienced redundancy in a recession.

I am convinced that other graduates will benefit from my experience.

Please note that the book is equally intended for both men and women. To remain neutral I considered using 'he' and 'she' but this read clumsily. The book therefore uses the single pronoun 'he' throughout in the hope it will make easier reading.

PART ONE
THE PLAN

Chapter 1

A Plan for a Job Search

The job market is highly competitive. A professional attitude makes the difference between a job and no job, between a good job and an ordinary one, and between a job sooner rather than later.

This book should reduce the time and effort required to learn about the job market and how to sell yourself in it. You will still have to work hard to be successful. However, if you first recognise that there is much to learn about the job search procedure, you will do less work in the long term.

The job search is a selling exercise in which you are the product and the employer is the customer. You must examine yourself, the product, to see which employer would be interested. Also, since in selling situations the customer has all the power, you should identify what each individual employer requires and adapt yourself to provide it. Do not expect an employer to take you just as you are.

Before forming a job search plan, recognise that progress falls into discrete stages. At each stage you have to make a certain amount of effort to succeed. To fail at any stage means starting again.

At each stage of the job search the employer will ask questions. A great deal of effort is required to prepare answers. You need to understand that some questions are leading questions. Employers cannot ask directly everything they want to know about you. They will infer certain things from other answers that you give, and the way that you give them. It is misleading when you do not know exactly why a question has been asked or what it is that the employer wants to know. Preparation is the key to success in this difficult communications exercise.

We all judge one another subjectively, making generalisations about personality traits based on groups of observations. This is also how employers weigh up job applicants. Most employers attempt to be as objective about the job selection procedure as they can. However, they are powerless to ignore the human and social aspects. After all, one of the most important things that an employee must do is to fit in and get on with his colleagues. Teamwork is very important, and hard to achieve.

Another important quality is that a candidate must *show* that he can do the job. Students expect their qualifications and training to prove this, but work experience is far more important in demonstrating ability. You need to practise talking about your experience and achievements in a way that shows you can do the job. Alternatively, you must convince an employer that you are capable of learning quickly.

Finally, candidates' appearance and values are expected to fall within expected norms. For certain jobs, men need to recognise that long hair and earrings on men will be noticed and taken into account when their appearance is weighed up. Your manners will be noticed and added to the equation. The longer your hair, the more acceptable you may need to be in other ways.

Perhaps the most frustrating part of a job search is the experience of repeated rejection, without knowing the reasons. I hope that the information provided in this book will allow candidates to review and reflect on their experiences in a positive way. A constructive learned approach will be successful in the end.

THE PLAN

If everything goes according to plan, you will

- identify how to convince someone to give you a job
- succeed in getting a job offer
- know how you did it, so as to be able to repeat it

The key to success is to work effectively at each stage of the job search.

Failure to have a plan invites failure to get the job. Unsuccessful interviews are unpleasant memories from which a candidate may wrongly conclude that he will never find a job. Worse, he might imagine that there is something wrong with him. Without a strategy, the candidate is less likely to succeed next time.

Someone who has a plan can review what went wrong if he does not get the job and can do better next time. He can put the experience down to chance, and therefore maintain high morale and self-esteem.

A structured approach to the job search is:

- preparation *then*
- opportunity *equals*
- a job offer

There are two reasons why candidates might, wrongly, look for opportunity before doing any preparation. First, they fear that opportunities are scarce and are afraid of missing one. They panic, making an inadequate attempt that is predestined to failure. Second, they are unaware of the preparation that is required and how to go about it.

It is important to recognise that finding a job requires much hard work. Done half-heartedly, it could take forever. The total effort needed becomes less the harder the job-seeker works. More effort for less time is the best approach. It generates a choice of job offers. Employers are also impressed by enthusiasm.

The job search is a staged process.

1. Decide what sort of job to do
2. Prepare a CV
3. Obtain an interview
4. Obtain a second interview
5. Secure the job offer

The job search is like a series of hurdles. Getting the job requires a huge effort at each successive jump. A common

7

mistake is to feel relieved after succeeding at one hurdle then fail to make enough effort at the next one. Candidates must never relax before the final hurdle has been cleared, else they face having to start again.

Stage 1: Decide what sort of job to do

What sort of job would you like? What things do you do well, and what things not so well? Many candidates will neglect this self-analysis completely. As a result they will lack direction and place themselves at a serious disadvantage with the competition.

If you are a final-year undergraduate you should ask friends and parents for their opinions about the sort of job they could imagine you doing. Perhaps give some thought to a higher degree at a different university. There is less competition to undertake higher degrees, and if you are academically minded, an MA or PhD at a prestigious university might be a worthwhile achievement. Consult your university careers adviser.

Preferably, final-year undergraduates should enter their final year with a clear aim.

Stage 2: Prepare a CV

The CV is an important personal sales document. Not to have one will disadvantage a candidate compared with the competition. Find the time and energy to do it.

The CV must be perfect. It develops as the job search progresses, as the candidate continually refines it. The best policy is to put effort into writing a good CV at the earliest opportunity.

Ideally, undergraduates should prepare their CVs before or during the October of their final year.

Stage 3: Obtain an interview

A good job, advertised nationally, attracts around 400 quality applications. Naïve candidates assume that if they make 400 applications then statistically they should get at least one interview. Informed or experienced ones know that this is not true. Anyone who continues to think that the law of averages has any relevance to a job search will take a long time to find a job.

Suppose an employer receives 400 applications. A person cannot read 400 CVs without mentally switching off. The covering letter is therefore crucial. If it does not sell the CV, then the chances of success are negligible. At this stage the candidate has to make an effort to prepare good covering letters relevant to each job that he applies for.

Sending out dozens of applications at a time is like using a shotgun. A shotgun fires lots of shot over a wide area but lacks sufficient power in any one direction. With the shotgun method you have to apply without knowing much about the jobs. A job hunt requires the opposite approach. Lots of power must be directed at a specific target. People resorting to shotgun tactics do so because they wrongly perceive that the job search is a numbers game. Unfortunately, employers are sensitive to it and do not like it. The employer needs to feel special. He wants to feel that he is the particular employer and this the particular job that the candidate really wants.

Stage 4: Obtain a second interview

A search and selection agency may interview a dozen people for one vacancy, or about twenty for three vacancies. The agency then forwards four to six CVs, with interview notes, to the employer. Such agencies want to do a good job and to get repeat business. Their immediate concern is to prepare some notes on the candidate to forward to the employer. Help the interviewer to prepare a good set of interview notes, and improve your chances of a second interview.

What does a convincing set of interview notes contain? It probably includes the candidate's key selling points, his main achievements to date, and his reasons for wanting to work with the employer in question. It is impossible for a candidate to help someone to prepare these notes if he could not prepare them himself.

Where the employer carries out his own short-listing interviews, for example on the milk round (see Chapter 10), the principle is the same.

Success at this stage depends on hard work and preparation.

Stage 5: Secure the job offer

Failure at the second interview is more upsetting than failure at the first. Expectations are raised by initial success, only to be destroyed at the last hurdle.

A job search in a recession lasts about nine months. At first, the candidate may be incapable of effective action. Later, he gets some first interviews. By the time he reaches a second interview the stakes are high. Failing a second interview is agony, a definition of despair. The experience, though, will teach anyone who has failed to prepare for an interview that he must prepare for future ones.

KNOW YOUR PRODUCT

Before you apply for a job, make sure it is really what you want to do.

Also, before you can convince an employer of your strengths, you yourself need to know what they are.

What things have you done well in the past? Are they the things that you enjoy doing and want to do for a living? Most of us like doing the things that we do well and which make us successful. However, we have to be realistic: very few people become top footballers, or get invited to host a travel show.

For those already working, to drag on with something you cannot do well is a misery. A long, hard think is needed. If you have already embarked on a career, the decision to change track is a tough one. Possibly such a decision follows the difficult admission that all is not well in your present position. Realising that you have been unsuccessful in a job is demoralising. But success is always relative, and a prerequisite for success is to have faith in ourselves. It is an emotional issue. Ask those you trust for their views on what you should do.

It is frequently supposed that a change in direction involves a drop in pay. If the possibilities are researched well enough the drop can be minimised. Normally, doing well at what you enjoy will make it worthwhile.

When you know what you want to do and what your strengths are, try to identify *where* you might work.

When you sell yourself, decide which aspects of yourself you will emphasise, and which you will avoid. Your CV, covering letter and performance at interview must all reflect your strengths relevant to the vacancy, and should not reveal your weaknesses.

In not revealing weaknesses, it is important not to tell lies. Conceal weaknesses by not allowing them to arise, not by deceit. Lies lead to trouble when you are found out. Plan to control the proceedings sufficiently well that the questions you might founder on never arise. This skill of presenting yourself in the best possible light does not come naturally, but with practice it is easy to develop.

Review your greatest successes: imagine talking to an employer about them; convince him that you could repeat them.

MARKET RESEARCH

Find out what is relevant first. You need to know about the company in order to plan which of your strengths you should stress in your CV, covering letter and interview. You should only stress relevant qualities and achievements.

There are a number of things you can do which will improve your chances of being offered the job, and of knowing whether

11

to accept it. Read the newspaper, especially the business pages. Evidence of some knowledge of the relevant sector makes a good impression at the interview, but not if overplayed so that it becomes transparent. Read professional journals to discover which companies are doing well and which ones badly. If professional journals contain job adverts, look through back issues. Some companies show up as having a recruitment problem. Find out why.

Job advertisements often contain useful information. When replying to an advert, read it repeatedly to make sure you do not miss anything. Where adverts give a source of further information, follow it up.

Sometimes job adverts provide a contact name and phone number. The contact might be a junior person whose job is to provide information. Alternatively, it could be the person who will choose between candidates.

If you speak to a secretary or personnel officer, try to gather as much information as possible. Find out the names of the people you would work for. Ask for any reports, accounts or sales brochures that might be relevant. Enquire if the job is a new one, or if not who did it last and what are they doing now. How long has the job been advertised?

If the person you speak to is more senior, he might well be involved in the interviewing process. Remember that he will recall your telephone call when he makes his decision. Think of the most significant message that you have and get it across during the conversation. The best way to pass on information is in reply to a question, because it is then that the other person is listening most closely. The sort of questions that might allow you to convey something important are:

- How did you hear about the vacancy?
- What is your current job?

What will you say in reply?

Above all, sound interested in the job.

Even if the advertisement does not invite you to telephone, it is a good idea to ring the switchboard. Choose a quiet time of day, avoiding lunchtime. Explain that you are applying for a job, and ask for the names of the key people and their job titles. Find out if there is someone in the company who could send the annual report or other information. Switchboard staff are normally trained to be helpful. They are the first point of contact between the company and the outside world. At any subsequent interview do not mention that you phoned, but if it is discovered by those with the authority to give you the job, the interest that you have shown will be welcomed. There are too many candidates who appear not to care less about where they are employed. You should plan to give the impression that this is the company you would most like to work for. It is awkward and unconvincing to say that outright, so it is important that you imply it by the things that you do: actions speak louder than words.

CUSTOMER FOCUS

Having identified a potential employer, find out all you can about them. Ask yourself:

- Who chooses the successful candidate?
- Why do they want someone to work for them?
- What are their selection criteria?
- How can I persuade them to choose me?

As a rule, these things are not explained by the company itself. However, it is easy enough to discover the answers, using a combination of questions and observation. Here is a starting point for each of the above questions:

Who chooses the successful candidate?

Normally for a technical or managerial job it is the person who will be your new boss. However, some other people have influence. In medium-sized and large companies, responsibility

13

is often shared. A panel of several departmental heads confer to make a decision. Normally the key person is the new boss, but he wants reassurance from his colleagues that they agree with his choice. Thus you have to sell yourself to a prospective new boss, and inspire confidence in his colleagues.

One person always involved, though sometimes imagined as wielding greater influence then he really does, is the company personnel manager. His strength is that he is familiar with the recruitment procedure, and he is often involved in passing completed application forms to the potential new boss and coordinating interview dates. On the day of the interview, the personnel manager might also help by informing candidates about administrative details such as salaries, pensions and benefits. As he does so, he inevitably forms a subjective impression of each candidate. You must not leave this impression to chance.

The candidate's self-esteem affects his impact on the personnel manager and all the other interviewers.

Why do they want someone to work for them?

When someone becomes a manager he has to find time to network and to communicate both within the organisation and outside. Thus he needs help with the detail of day-to-day operations. Bosses want to hold all the power and authority for their part of the organisation, whilst delegating practical responsibilities to people they can trust.

They are looking for people like them. In addition they want people who are reliable, intelligent and enthusiastic, people who can do the job.

What are their selection criteria?

It is frustrating for the candidate not to know precisely what the employer wants. However, it is the same for all the other candidates. Those who think about it ahead of an interview do better. Sometimes interviewers have a checklist, which might contain the following points:

- Personality
- Ability to work with others
- Achievements
- Intelligence
- Hobbies and interests

This is a useful list, but it does not explain what the interviewer really wants. He is actually looking for someone he likes, someone who is like him, and someone he can get on with. The candidate must be able to do the job. Employers are also interested in employing clever people. As a result, intelligence and personality testing is popular.

How can I persuade them to choose me?

The interviewer is always making inferences and weighing up the candidates. You can take advantage of this process to create a good impression and to convince the interviewer that you can do the job and fit in well with existing employees.

You will prepare a CV and covering letter that are easy to read and relevant to the vacancy. At interview, you dress conservatively, speak well and display good manners. You have appropriate values, are ambitious and hard-working. You say that if offered the job you would take it. There is no reason why you should not get the job.

WORK ON MORE THAN ONE SELLING OPPORTUNITY

Plan your job search properly and you should be able to choose between a number of offers. You can only do this by working on several opportunities simultaneously. While one is at the application form stage, others may be at the first and second interview stages.

Ideally, if you get several offers close enough together, you can afford to turn down a poor opportunity.

POSITIVE REFLECTION

After a rejection, and after each interview, candidates can review the experience and try to extract some learning points. It is better to review things positively and try to build on your strengths than to dwell on any weaknesses.

It is not necessarily your fault if you did not get the job. Another candidate impressed the interviewers more: how did he do it? Perhaps he was better prepared, had identified his key selling points more clearly and primed the interviewer to ask the right questions. Maybe he had found out more about the company and impressed in that way.

Search for the things that went well and aim to repeat them next time. Did the interviewer give any hint about why you had been invited to the interview? If so, can you use it to get further interviews? Did you feel that you got on well with any of the interviewers, and if so why? Could you do that again in the future? Were your strengths relevant to the job vacancy? If not, how can you make sure that in future they are?

Naturally everyone is concerned about their weaknesses, and as we grow older most of us become more aware of what these are. However, a weakness cannot be turned into a strength. Candidates have to talk about their positive qualities and avoid revealing their negative points. Ideally, you should look for jobs where your weaknesses are not important. The only thing you then need do about them is fail to mention them.

There are a number of easily recognisable mistakes that candidates make at interviews:

- **Talking too much**. Candidates should talk eloquently about their achievements and strengths in reply to the interviewer's questions. Aimless chattering counts against them. This applies equally during the evening meal, factory visit or lunchtime chat parts of the selection procedure.
- **Falling for the deliberate pause**. A trained interviewer might use a pause to encourage a candidate to say more. He hopes that the candidate will tell what he ought not to. Beware of this, and do not be afraid of silence.

- **Overfamiliarity**. Candidates who are overfamiliar or arrogant can get rejected for this reason alone. It is easy to make the mistake of sitting before you are invited to, removing a jacket, smoking or calling someone by their first name without being asked.
- **Wrong body language**. Nervous body language or fidgeting can spoil the rapport between interviewer and candidate.
- **Dress and appearance**. Remove five o'clock shadow, excess or flashy jewellery, etc.
- **Criticising a previous employer**. Future employers suspect that the candidate will say the same about them.

Chapter 2

Reviewing Your Skills

What are your transferable skills like? How will you get them across using your CV and covering letter, and at the interview?

The phrase 'transferable skills' refers to the list of personal competencies required by managers. This will include:

- concern for standards
- concern for efficiency
- commitment to the job
- self-confidence
- thinking skills
- evaluating information
- understanding others
- concern for impact
- assertiveness
- communication skills

You will demonstrate these skills by talking to your interviewer about your personal achievements. Decide which transferable skills are your strong points that you can sell to an employer. Can you anticipate which ones the interviewer will be particularly interested in? Which ones are especially relevant to the job vacancy?

Concern for standards

Walking around a building site or factory, it is common to see posters urging workers to have pride in the job and to get it right first time. Redoing a job doubles its cost. In addition there is the knock-on cost of the delay and lost goodwill caused by sending shoddy goods to the customer. Awareness of this additional cost has increased significantly. The Japanese managed to avoid sending out faulty products, which resulted in British goods temporarily losing their reputation for quality.

The right-first-time idea applies equally to services.

Some quality initiatives introduced to raise standards in Britain talk of 'zero defects'. All quality initiatives require measurement of nonconformity and a commitment to reducing it. Most people naturally derive satisfaction from a job well done and readily accept these ideas. However, there are a few people who do not feel the need to achieve excellence, and they can have a detrimental effect on the rest of the workforce. Therefore, not taking on such people in the first place is a high priority for an employer.

An example of where a concern for standards can be vital is in safety at work. Those who consider standards unimportant are likely to become a liability when they neglect to report faulty equipment, refuse to follow rigorous procedures or simply leave things lying around. No one wants to work with them.

Closely allied to the concern-for-standards competency is the fact that many people are 'results-oriented'. Such people are anxious to conclude a task successfully, and want to see a measurable benefit from their efforts. Sometimes results orientation and a concern for standards can seem mutually exclusive. This is because someone in a hurry to achieve might conceivably take short cuts. In a job search the two qualities are not at all incompatible. The candidate has to firmly establish both, not one or the other.

The interviewer may ask questions aimed at discovering the candidate's views on such things as quality initiatives and permits to work. The candidate is expected to reply with a mixture of fact and opinion. His talk about previous experience must show awareness of standards, and he should convey to the interviewer his belief in high standards.

Concern for efficiency

Concern for efficiency is about how a job is done. The best possible efficiency is achieved by applying methods and procedures correctly. The interviewer wants to know that the candidate thinks about how things are done and contributes to make procedures effective.

Employers do not want their workforce to waste valuable time. When an employee becomes a manager, he is responsible for other people's time. He should not be the sort of person who wastes time, resources or money.

Concern for efficiency can be complementary to concern for standards and results orientation.

Commitment to the job

Any employer is most interested in people who will work hard. The interviewer wants to know if the candidate will stay late to finish a job before an important deadline. At a more senior level he needs to find out the extent to which the candidate will take work home with him. The employer wants to know if the candidate shares his feeling of devotion to work. This could be crucial to how someone gets on with their boss. People who are devoted to their work find it irritating when others behave frivolously. Bosses are often bosses because they have shown commitment to the job.

People who are committed to the job see extra work as a challenge and enjoy doing it. If they discover new things that need doing they take ownership of them. Conversely, people lacking commitment ignore additional work that crops up. They pretend that it does not exist or assume that someone else will do it. Candidates need to think of examples where they took on extra work in addition to the assignments they were asked to do. Ideally they should explain how they showed initiative in appropriating work for themselves.

If people are committed to their job they find out how it fits in with the company's activities as a whole. This makes them feel that they are involved in something bigger, and gives them satisfaction when the company succeeds. They tend to be rewarded by being given demanding mainstream activities. Those not committed to their work are often marginalised, by being given undemanding, nonessential jobs. Candidates should explain how their previous employers trusted them with high-profile assignments.

Commitment to the job is hard for an interviewer to predict because it is circumstantial. It is important to try and show commitment to a previous job using a work example. New graduates can show commitment to their studies or chosen profession. Commitment can also be demonstrated by talking about relevant extracurricular activities.

Self-confidence

Self-confidence means maintaining a positive belief in yourself. Faced with problems, self-confident people have faith that they can succeed. People with self-confidence see challenges as opportunities rather than threats. They have a can-do mentality and are not afraid to have a go. They will persevere when others give up.

People with self-confidence are an asset to an organisation: their enthusiasm and positive belief can encourage others to continue.

Thinking skills

Organisations want to know about a candidate's general intelligence. It is common for the personnel manager to ask the candidate to complete an intelligence test. The candidate might be told that the test is unimportant, and that the results are not used in the selection process, but this is untrue.

While exam results might be an initial indication of intelligence, most people accept that excellent results can be achieved by intensive coaching. Specially designed intelligence tests can measure analytical and conceptual thinking skills.

You should not be surprised if you are asked to do one of these tests. The best preparation is to have a good sleep the night before. Read the instructions carefully. Make sure the rules are clear. For example, are penalty points deducted for wrong answers? Attempt all the questions, possibly leaving the most difficult ones until last.

Evaluating information

It is important for managers to be able to evaluate information. This means understanding and remembering what the content of a report is, and deciding whether it is useful in the context of previous information.

One intelligence test that candidates may be asked to sit is designed to assess their ability to evaluate information. This test consists of a passage of information followed by a list of statements. The candidate has to say which of the statements are true, which are not true, and which are impossible to tell. The test is subject to a time limit.

Understanding others

There is a definite skill to perceiving how others feel, and understanding their point of view. This skill is associated with straightforward intelligence. Therefore people who behave inconsiderately are sometimes thought ignorant.

Understanding others involves tact and diplomacy, in addition to a willingness to put oneself in the other person's position. It means bothering to think about other people's points of view. This skill is best shown by talking about relevant experience.

Understanding others is a critical skill in getting people to do things; in other words in managing them. It is vital to any teamwork where understanding the group's aims and sharing commitment is important.

Concern for impact

How others perceive us is more important at work than how we really are. It is very difficult to ascertain, let alone control, how others see us.

In companies with an 'organic' management structure, direct line management is not the norm. Such companies like to recruit managers who have a 'management presence'. These are people who, on entering a room, immediately become the focus of attention, as if they are in charge. People who have a management presence somehow often seem to take up more space than others. They tend to speak slowly and articulately, after due consideration, and to listen more than they talk. In conversation they contribute noticeably less than the other person, give away less about how they feel, and speak more in terms of facts than opinions.

In contrast people with little management presence habitually give away their personal authority by giggling, smiling inappropriately, apologising unnecessarily and rambling on in conversation.

The way a person dresses influences his impact on others. At work it is important to dress in the same way as your peers in order to be accepted. At a job interview, it is equally important to fit in by dressing in the expected way. In any situation it is better to dress tidily than it is to be shabby or over-casual.

Although dress and body language create first impressions, and first impressions are lasting ones, it is a genuine concern for impact that maintains long-term work relationships.

Assertiveness

Most people recognise that assertiveness is a personal skill, and for some it can even be a preoccupation.

Non-assertive, passive behaviour, is not standing up for one's rights and failing to ask for what one wants. It is being unable to refuse unreasonable requests. It leads people into trouble because others eventually cannot understand them and do not know what to expect from them. Other people find it difficult to get along with passive behaviour, and so sometimes avoid passive people. Passive people are often aware of their behaviour, and it is possible for them to change.

Over-assertive behaviour is aggressive. Aggression involves denying people their rights. It does not matter whether this is intentional or not. Aggressive people often cannot see that their behaviour is unacceptable, and thus they find it hard to change.

Assertive behaviour can be learned, and most local colleges run evening classes. They teach a basic set of behavioural tools with which to tackle common situations. These are practised in role-playing exercises, which can be repeated at home if required.

Strangely, being naturally assertive will not be a particular help at most job interviews. This is because the candidate is not expected to be in control. However, if the interviewer behaves aggressively, the candidate has to be both assertive and diplomatic. If an aggressive interviewer asks a question the candidate would rather not answer, the assertive response is to reply to a different, unasked question. This is how politicians get round awkward issues. If the interviewer asks a string of personal or irrelevant questions the candidate should explain that he is not sure how to answer. He should ask why the interviewer wants to know these things.

Communication skills

Completing application forms, writing CVs and covering letters, and talking at interviews all display a candidate's communication skills. Candidates are judged by the neatness and eloquence of their applications.

Communication skills are so important in the job search that sometimes employers choose the person with the best skills in this area instead of the one who would be the best for the job. Here are some tips:

- Application forms often ask candidates to use black ink and write in their normal handwriting. Do this anyway. The neatness of the application form is the first impression an employer gets. Any letter accompanying the application form or CV should be written in black ball-point pen on plain A4 paper. If a letter is particularly long it may be typewritten to help the reader. However, typed letters are not as personal, and their presentation is less persuasive than a neatly handwritten letter. Typed letters suggest mass production and so if used should be carefully personalised.
- Where it is possible to use a diagram to convey information more precisely this should be considered. Diagrams are a

very visual way to communicate and are sufficiently rare to attract attention in the context of a job search. Used appropriately, diagrams are impressive.

- Writing skills also include selecting the content of the application so that it is all relevant to the job on offer. Irrelevant material is a distraction and dilutes the message. The opportunity to get your strong points over is too precious to squander.
- Draft the application form before filling it in neatly. Try to read the draft through the eyes of the recipient not the sender. Any alterations?
- Rehearse what to say at the interview.

Chapter 3

Personality

Thinking about the sort of person you are will help you work out what type of job would suit you. Potential employers will almost certainly do this, so it is important that you do it first. Most jobs, particularly managerial posts, require teamwork skills. There are limits to what an individual can achieve. Each person must fit in to the team environment of a modern organisation in order to contribute to its collective success. The skills involved are more than just personal ones.

Ideally, you should have some knowledge about the different teamwork personalities, and know the one, or ones, which apply to you. Above all, it is important to understand how you behave in a team environment. This will determine whether other people accept your ideas, like you and get on with you, and whether you will be considered line management material. Personnel may ask a candidate to complete a personality test, and the interviewer will also infer things from the answers to certain questions. The employer's objective is to take on particular types of team player, and to avoid others.

In all this, it is important to face the selection procedure with high self-esteem.

WHAT SORTS OF PERSONALITIES ARE THERE?

The most common classification of personality is the distinction between introvert and extrovert behaviour. This is the way in which people handle one another. It is a widely held belief that someone must be either an introvert or an extrovert, never both. In reality it is not so simple. There are degrees of introvert and extrovert behaviour, with most people falling somewhere between the two. Also, an introvert can pass as an extrovert on occasion, by using acquired social skills to be outgoing and friendly, while an extrovert can be perceived as an introvert if he is particularly restrained. It is hard to make an accurate appraisal based on a brief encounter, especially if the situation is an artificial one, such as a job interview.

People also have different ways of handling information and organising their work. Some people are creative. Others are more practical. Someone who is creative might have lots of clever ideas about how to solve a problem. It is the practical person who will translate the ideas into action and complete the job. In the team environment, both types of people are needed. However, creative people often sit back and watch what is going on, while the more practical team members take an active interest in the detail of producing results. Consequently, practical people tend to take the credit. Generally, practical people who push for results are the people who get promoted to line management positions. At board level, the abilities to see the big picture and to extrapolate information become important. These are the strengths of the creative individual. However, very few reach board level.

Creative people may find it frustrating to work in a team environment because inevitably most of their ideas are rejected. Other team members may resent their intelligence and wish that the creative person would make a more practical contribution. Therefore, employers sometimes reject creative people in favour of practical types who will fit in more easily.

Behaviour may change over time. If you read a good book on teamwork you will become aware of the manner in which your personality could develop to improve your career prospects.

RELATING JOB TO PERSONALITY

The correlation of personality type to job suitability is achieved by asking existing employees to complete personality profile tests. The completed tests are then compared to find which sorts of people are doing which jobs. However, there is inevitably considerable overlap. The same job can be done by different sorts of people. There will also be some uncertainty about what sort of person you are. Final-year undergraduates may be too young or inexperienced to determine their own personalities. I recommend that you read a textbook on teamwork so that you can make an informed decision. The following simplified view provides an introduction:

- Practical people often make good team players. They should join an organisation and work in a team. They might consider jobs in production or construction.
- People who are creative and full of imagination could find teamwork frustrating. Other team members could find them frustrating, too. On the other hand, they can do jobs requiring individual flair. If prepared to carry their ideas to completion, they will want to be judged on their individual achievements. Suitable jobs include market analyst, teacher, writer or salesperson. Jobs in research also require creative people.
- Those neither full of individual flair nor good at organising other people may prefer to take a supporting role. Fellow team members appreciate them. Many teams contain too few helpful personalities. These people may progress to administrative positions.

COMPLETING PERSONALITY TESTS

Personality testing is a specialist job, and varying levels of complexity are used. Personality profile tests ask broadly similar questions in different ways. This is for two reasons. First, the tests look for groups of responses that agree and together confirm a particular personality trait. Second, by asking the same sort of thing more than once, cross-checking is possible to make sure that the answers are consistent.

The candidate does the test quickly and has no time to cross-check his own answers. The tester has a prepared list of cross-checks and plenty of time. There is a real chance that outright lies will be detected, so candidates should always be truthful.

When we think of someone we know, we immediately generalise about some of their personality traits with such adjectives as friendly, clever, proud, creative, lively, persistent. It is only those personality traits which consistently lie outside a broad norm that are remembered. In the same way, personality tests look for groups of replies that, when taken together, suggest a trait that is out of the ordinary.

The instructions might ask candidates to avoid giving middle-of-the-road answers. If all a candidate's answers are middle-of-the-road it will be impossible to tell anything from the test. However, from the candidate's point of view, it is highly dangerous to give positive replies that could suggest a false personality trait. Candidates should give answers that are as accurate as possible. If the middle-of-the-road answer is correct then that is the answer to give.

Some things to look out for:

Assertiveness

Assertiveness is another desirable personality trait. It is difficult to test objectively as it will depend on a person's self-esteem and on the circumstances. High self-esteem is particularly important in a job application because it generates a positive attitude. A question on assertiveness might be: 'If someone says something you do not agree with, would you speak out?' It is best to say that you would, if, of course, that is the truth.

Instability

A candidate must avoid appearing mentally unstable. Asked 'Would you react angrily if someone ignored you completely?' you should say that you would not! It is unfair that in the stressful situation of a job interview an accidental wrong reply to a question like this is completely damning. On the other hand, it is important for employers not to take on unstable personalities.

Casualness

Casualness is the opposite of a concern for standards, and so it is undesirable. Questions to test for casualness are hard to spot, but might appear in the form: 'Do some people say you are irresponsible?' The candidate should avoid agreeing.

Intelligence

Intelligence is desirable. As well as the specific intelligence tests, there might be intelligence questions in the general personality test. These have proper answers, and do not ask for a preference. Getting them right is a sign of intelligence. These questions test your concentration. Spot questions that require a factual answer for what they are, slow down, and get them right.

SELF-ESTEEM

Self-esteem affects the way people respond to situations. In particular, high self-esteem makes it possible to cope with the unexpected in a positive way. In a job search it is crucial to be able to react to surprises in a way which treats the new circumstance as an opportunity and not a threat.

Redundancy is an event that could trigger an extended period of low self-esteem. Even if it is due only to the declining fortunes of the company, redundancy is likely to be a severe blow to your self-esteem. In this situation it is important to concentrate on the job search and to avoid dwelling on the past. Instead, work hard to develop and improve your CV and covering letter.

The interview

The interviewer will make a subjective appraisal of the sort of person a candidate is. No matter how suitable the candidate is on paper, it is the impression made on the interviewer that counts. High self-esteem at the time of the interview makes a key difference to the impression. High self-esteem comes over as a 'can-do' attitude, a concern for standards and an alert manner. These are all qualities that the interviewer will be looking for.

Conversely, candidates with low self-esteem are self-defeating. Typically they are waiting to admit to something terrible, agree that they probably could not do the job and reveal that there is something wrong with them.

Psychologists have noticed that self-esteem is cyclic. Any individual might have high self-esteem one day and low the next. Commonly a person has two or three days when he feels positive and able to cope, followed by two or three days when he does not. This is especially true of the unemployed. You should try to socialise on days when your self-esteem is high and avoid socialising when it is low. The job interview will ideally coincide with a day of high self-esteem.

Low self-esteem

Low self-esteem affects everyone from time to time. The key thing is not to let it influence your relationships with others. Your self-esteem may improve if you tell someone who is close to you what you are thinking.

Some things to avoid:

- Excessive alcohol consumption simply does not work.
- Keeping feelings pent-up inside is a mistake. In a crisis such as redundancy, people tend to do things to make matters worse. Any new crisis created may well eclipse the old one, but will not take it away. Facing a crisis constructively begins by accepting what has happened, and that it is a crisis. Express feelings of anger and bitterness when they apply.
- It is counterproductive to complain to anyone other than close friends or family. Never do anything to prevent a previous employer giving you a good reference. Normally an ex-employer will be pleased to provide a reference, and this should not be an additional worry. Even if personal

31

relationships become uncomfortable towards the end of your employment, you can still expect a good reference.

Avoid put-downs

In theory, self-esteem is a combination of self-confidence and self-respect.

Your self-confidence will improve when you review your achievements. It is reassuring to recognise past successes. Include both your professional and your personal achievements. Work out why they were special, what problems they involved, and how the problems were overcome.

Self-respect is something everyone has until they give it away. Do not believe that other people are always better than you in some way. Keep on telling yourself that you are a worthwhile person. If self-respect is a problem for you, here is a checklist of ways to improve it:

- Make a list of people who tend to put you down in conversation. These people are bolstering their own self-respect at your expense. Jealous colleagues who have developed the knack of witty remarks are the worst sort. Limit your exposure to these people. Write down and remember the steps to take that will reduce your contact with them.
- List the ways in which you can end conversations with people you wish to avoid. The following phrases may be helpful:

  'I'm really busy right now'
  'I will speak to you another time'
  'That is very interesting but I must be going now'

- List the derogatory remarks that people make. Normally there are only a handful but they recur. Make up an answer for each, and rehearse them.
- Smart dress and neat appearance help the development of self-respect. Keep clean and tidy, well groomed and well mannered.

Chapter 4

Choosing Your Job

Changing your job is an opportunity to change the direction of your career, for better or for worse. Faced with unemployment, the choice appears to be between work and redundancy. This is not true. Thinking positively, the correct approach is to spend some time considering which job to do and then to work very hard to get that particular job. A person prepared to take any job at all appears defeatist. This shows up, particularly at interview, and leads to rejection. Conversely the person who knows exactly what he wants, and why, appears positive. He is more likely to be successful. At the very least, knowing what you want, and why, helps you to answer some difficult interview questions. For example, you will be asked:

- Why do you want to work here?
- What are your strengths?
- Which of your strengths are relevant to this vacancy?

BIG OR SMALL COMPANY?

In a big company a new employee will be a small fish in a big pond. He will find it hard to make any impact on the mainstream activity of the organisation or to influence its direction. If the company is poorly managed there is little he can do to improve things. A new employee has to work hard at ingratiating himself with his boss, and his actual job performance might not appear to be very important. An employee who gets on well with the boss in a big company can expect promotion to a higher position than someone who works for a small outfit.

In a small company the new employee will be a big fish in a small pond. He will quickly become involved in the day-to-day mainstream activities of the company. His job performance will be important to the continued growth and success of the firm. He has more opportunity to achieve things and to make a noticeable contribution than he would in a big company. But while the level of responsibility given to a new employee in a small firm will be greater in the first place, promotion will depend on the continued expansion of the company, and on the individual's job performance. Promotion from within is the norm in a small firm because new bosses have to have a good knowledge of the company, its technology, markets and products.

Experience in a big company early in a career is an asset if the company has a good training scheme. It is also beneficial if the company moves graduates around to give them experience. However, who wants to have to leave after a few years to capitalise on this experience?

Experience with a small company at the start of a career will give a person early responsibility and the opportunity to achieve. However, it may be harder to move from a small company to a big one than the other way around because of the training issue.

Big companies offer greater short-term job security because they are less likely to cease trading. They often have longer periods of notice and greater benefits if they do make people redundant. Small companies offer greater potential for long-term growth and security. In general, small companies offer the prospect of growth and big ones that of decline. However, some small companies are wholly owned by poorly managed larger holding companies. The small company will suffer with any downturn that befalls the parent company. When a holding company falters, redundancy programmes extend across the whole of the conglomerate.

Big companies often have good pension schemes. The company might contribute between 10 per cent and 30 per cent of gross salary to a company pension scheme. Of course, some of the benefit from this is lost if the employee is made redundant or leaves before the age of 50. After 50, it is possible to have a reduced pension beginning immediately. The greater chance of being made redundant after this age is offset by the pension benefit enjoyed as a result. Most schemes are based on final salary. Employees who leave at an early stage in their career, when still on a lower salary, lose some of the value of their years' service. This fact will often hold an employee to a company where prospects are poor when he should be developing his career elsewhere. Personal pensions, supposed to solve the problem, are unattractive because employers will not make realistic contributions to them. High-flying directors negotiate a good contribution to a personal pension, but ordinary employees cannot.

SPECIALISATION

Most people enjoy what they are good at and this leads them to specialise. This should result in better pay and job satisfaction.

Some qualifications and experience lead to a natural vocation. Following a vocational career with qualifications often pays well. To try something different probably means accepting less money. However, the drop in salary may be less than expected and the new opportunities may be worth it. The option to change vocation is open mainly to young unmarried people with no family responsibility and to people retiring early with a company pension. Police officers and footballers, retiring while youthful, often begin second careers. People starting second careers generally have the wisdom to choose something they enjoy. Those starting a career for the first time should also give thought to what they enjoy doing.

What successes can you repeat? What are the worst failures that must be avoided? Which specialisation satisfies both criteria?

SALARY VERSUS PROSPECTS

Some jobs offer a good salary at the outset, while others, which pay less well to begin with have better prospects later on. This is what building a career is all about. Students forgo the opportunity of earning money for three or four years in the expectation of a better salary later. More people are studying in further education, and the world of employment is becoming increasingly competitive, with the number of unskilled jobs falling and the number of careers requiring further education and training increasing.

A job that appears to offer better prospects is only worth considering when the certainty of the prospects materialising is extremely high. Deceit in respect of the likelihood of certain prospects is widespread. Arguably, the candidate's safest option is to choose the job with the highest initial salary. All increases from then on are based on the healthy starting salary.

When looking for a job the candidate is marketing his skills, and it is therefore appropriate for him to demand as much money as he is able.

TIME TO MOVE ON?

The decision to move from a company is a difficult one and not to be taken lightly. People are the same the world over. Never make the mistake of expecting things to be better elsewhere. The grass is never greener on the other side of the fence.

The main reason for changing your job is to improve your personal market value through good experience. At the same time, by remarketing yourself, you can get a pay rise.

Employees must be able to look back on their careers and show a record of achievement in each job they have held. Moving too often can mean failing to do anything really significant anywhere. This will reduce a person's market value. A record of frequent moves can be detrimental. A prospective employer might suspect that the candidate has

36

been forced to leave each time because he could not do the job.

Early in a career it is possible to move and find that it has been a mistake. The new job is not as expected. However, a series of mistakes is fatal, because the career history built up will lack both achievement and direction.

It is wise to move, at any stage in a career, when redundancy looms. Leave sooner than be made redundant. When it is clear that the end is coming, find a new employer at the earliest opportunity. It is easier to get another job if you are still working, and in addition the psychological damage of redundancy cannot be overestimated. Finding a new job is always possible, although in a recession it takes great time and effort.

CHOOSING BETWEEN JOBS

It is important for an employer to choose the right candidate. It is even more important for a candidate to choose the right employer. A company employs many people. A candidate has only one job, and the wrong choice is a personal disaster.

Before deciding to take a job, you need to find out who your new boss will be. Is he someone you will like and get on with? Will he treat you properly, giving you worthwhile assignments?

You also need to know if the company is making a profit. Unless you will be in a position to reverse the situation, it is a mistake to take a job with an ailing company. Sometimes vacancies arise because other people have left the company to avoid redundancy.

You also need to give a little thought to how the new job will affect your family life. Is the location acceptable to the other members of the family? Does the job involve long or unsocial hours, and how will this alter life outside work? Finally, are there any health hazards, such as toxic chemicals or noise?

Chapter 5

Professional Help

New graduates beginning a job search for the first time are green, and do not know it. For people made redundant in a recession, it will seem a long haul back to employment. They are not expecting it. Both types of job-searcher could benefit from professional help.

There are two kinds of help. The first, free at university careers services, is expert advice on preparing a CV, and perhaps training in interview technique. The second is outplacement through an agency. Normally, outplacement is expensive. The fee is a percentage of the first year's salary. The help that outplacement agencies can provide will not be discussed here in detail: this book anticipates that candidates want to do the maximum for themselves.

Some companies pay for ex-employees to have outplacement help in finding a new job. This is sensitive and supporting, and is the very least a company should do if an employee has been made redundant. Otherwise, candidates need to make the effort for themselves. Facing unemployment makes even the most reasonable fees seem extortionate. Good help is going to be extraordinarily expensive. New graduates, who may have built up debts while studying, will not be able to afford to pay.

When professional help is available you should take it within the context of your own job search. You should not abandon your own plan or attempt to put the onus on someone else. For example, it is your responsibility to decide what to mention in your career history. Over time, you will want to refine and improve this carefully prepared introductory statement.

Whoever is on your side in the job search, no one knows you like you know yourself. You are the person best qualified to help. Finding a job is a matter more of effort than of expense.

PREPARING A CV

It takes much effort to produce a well-laid-out and grammatically correct CV. Professional help is available, advertised in the same places as job adverts. However, this is something that most graduates can do for themselves. A good word processor and high-quality printer are indispensable. Once on file, the CV can be edited and refined later.

A professional critique of your CV is worth considering. Undergraduates might ask a university careers adviser to comment. Some professional organisations, such as the American Institute of Chemical Engineers, offer this service free to members. There is no obligation to accept their suggestions.

INTERVIEW TECHNIQUE

A professional trainer helps a candidate to develop his interview technique by conducting mock interviews in front of a video camera. The trainer will help to prepare a career history for the candidate to recite early in the interview. It should lead to a series of positive questions which will allow the candidate to give well-rehearsed accounts of key achievements.

Performing serious mock interviews on video is the best possible preparation for the real thing. Nothing is more reassuring during an interview than to be able to think: 'I know the answer to this question and have rehearsed it.' That frees up thinking time and allows you to answer even difficult questions without a second thought. It also gives you time to run through a mental check list of your strong points. Which ones still have to be explained? Thinking time allows you to remain guarded about your weaknesses, and gives you the opportunity to absorb information about the company.

A friend with a video camera could substitute for professional help and is cheaper. However, you cannot always expect a friend to help you prepare your replies to the various questions that may arise.

Help with interview technique would be useful at any stage. It is probably most valuable to those people who have failed several interviews and who realise that they are doing something wrong. Anyone who has a record of interview failure should get help. A professional will quickly spot the problem, provide constructive support, and help to rebuild confidence.

PROFESSIONAL HELP TO AVOID

Any help offered by a third party, such as a recruitment agency, should be treated with caution. Why are they offering to help? It is not because they feel sympathetic. Normally, this help takes place over the telephone. The recruitment agency discusses the job situation. They may offer to put you on their books. In reality, the agency is using the opportunity to weigh you up. They want to see if any of the jobs on their records might be suitable.

In this situation you are working in the dark. You have no idea which of your strengths is relevant, and you do not know which achievements you should use to sell yourself. Furthermore, the agency has probably misled you as to the purpose of the conversation. You need to know what the job requires before you can persuade someone that you could do it.

Recruitment agents do not have the job-seeker's interests at heart. If they want to talk, it is to see if they have a relevant vacancy. You need to turn this situation around. It is important not to allow the agency to gain control. You can stay in charge by asking to be informed of any vacancies the agency has. Promise to contact them if any of these seem relevant. Say no more.

Once a recruitment agency knows of a candidate and has assessed his potential, it will be hard to alter that impression.

PART TWO
THE JOB APPLICATION

Chapter 6

Writing a CV

A curriculum vitae is a biographical account of a candidate's life. It is normal to use the abbreviation CV in conversation and in writing.

The CV is a job-seeker's personal sales document. Normally it is sent in reply to an advertisement together with a handwritten covering letter. Sample CVs and a covering letter are appended to this chapter (and are fictitious). The CV must be the best achievable advertisement. It has to be carefully thought out so that it creates a good impression. Although it should be totally accurate, it does not have to describe everything about the candidate.

All the candidate's time in education and at work must be accounted for. Therefore, it is useful to compose the CV in chronological sections. The degree of detail included in each section is up to the writer. Usually you only include the positive aspects of your career history.

A CV must be easy to read and immaculately typed on white A4 paper. It must not contain a single spelling or typographical error. It should be neatly folded in three and posted first class in a plain white envelope. The envelope must be addressed clearly in black ink, giving any reference provided in the advertisement. These simple rules reduce the chance of casual rejection. Often, CVs develop and improve as the job search progresses. Preparing a good CV takes time and effort, not easily afforded at the beginning of the job search. However, it is worth making a special effort to produce a polished CV at an early stage.

The CV is a very important document. You hope that when someone reads your CV they will invite you to an interview. The CV may then be used as an agenda for the interview and is referred to throughout the recruitment process. After the interview it is crucial when deciding whether to make a job offer.

When an advertisement specifically asks applicants to complete an application form then the application form *must* be used. Normally a company supplies its own form. Exceptionally, final-year undergraduates may be asked to submit a standard application form, which is available from university careers offices. Use your CV to cross-check that each important selling point appears on the form.

The CV is the accepted way to tell an employer about your career history. However, sometimes a letter might work just as well. For a new graduate, or someone near the beginning of their career, it is acceptable to combine in a letter those things normally included in a CV and covering letter. This alternative approach shows a personal touch and may help to convince the employer of a particular interest in the company. Handwritten career histories need to be immaculately written in black ink on A4 paper. A long, scruffy handwritten letter will put the reader off.

PREPARATION

If you are following a reasonable plan for a job search you will already have thought about your main achievements, strengths and selling points. You need to do so before you can begin your CV. Next identify which strengths are relevant to the type of job required, and choose the achievements that demonstrate these strengths. These achievements will be used in your CV and covering letter, and at the interviews. They will convince employers that you can do the job, are self-motivated, reliable, and so on. It is unlikely that all the achievements appearing in your CV can be identified at once. Therefore you should prepare a list over several days.

For each achievement used as an example of a personal strength, you need a record of what you did and what the result was. This information must be committed to memory, available for use throughout the various stages of the job search. Here is a sample record of an achievement:

Welded a limpet cooling coil to a reactor

I evaluated the performance of the existing cooling jacket by taking plant measurements. Then I calculated that improved cooling would be obtained using an internal cooling coil or an external limpet coil. I made outline designs for three options identified by discussion with my boss. They were:

1. *a bayonet cooler inserted through the vessel man-way*
2. *a cooling coil, which could be installed in pieces through the man-way*
3. *a limpet cooling coil*

I discussed the options with my boss. It was important to avoid water entering the reaction mixture. The best option to prevent water getting into the reactor was a limpet cooling coil. However, it was difficult to weld on a limpet coil because the vessel was made of thin stainless steel. I found out how to design the coil by referring to BS5500, designing it as if it was a stayed jacket. I sent copies of my design to the insurers for approval. I accompanied the insurance inspector to witness the weld procedure test at the welding contractor's premises. The initial tests were unsatisfactory: if the tests had been neglected, the vessel would have been ruined. Later I liaised with the contractor to complete the work during the annual shutdown. The result was even better than anticipated, and saved at least two hours of the batch time, worth up to £1m a year.

Strengths displayed: getting on with the boss, hands-on experience, and ability to evaluate alternative courses of action.

You might think of about five main achievements, avoiding repetition. Each example will support your claim to be an achiever. What strengths does each achievement demonstrate? Ideally, each new achievement should show different assets. However, nothing should be discarded. The more selling points and supporting material you have, the stronger your position.

The above sample record could be used to demonstrate equally any one of the three strengths. The requirements of the job vacancy must be identified. The achievement is then used to display whichever strength is the most relevant.

LAYOUT

The layout of your CV must be clear, concise and fluent. It helps the reader if you put the information in the order in which they expect it. Use a series of bold headings so that information can be found easily. Here are some examples:

- Background (Introduction)
- Present Job
- Career History (Work Experience)
- Education and Qualifications
- Personal

There are two forms of CV. One lists work experience in chronological order, or reverse chronological order, giving the dates for each job. The other form itemises experience by the type of work regardless of the employer, such as:

- Sales
- Purchasing
- Team Leadership

It is possible to use this second type of CV to hide gaps in an employment history, or to disguise frequent job changes. Usually an employer will want to check the continuity of the candidate's employment history. If there is time unaccounted for, the employer needs reassuring that the candidate was not in prison, in hospital under drug rehabilitation, etc. If redundant for a period, the interviewer wants to know why the candidate was made redundant.

I recommend a short introduction stating your most important strengths. A recent graduate or final-year undergraduate might then list his qualifications. Qualifications are a recent graduate's most important achievements. Next he should list any holiday jobs, followed by his hobbies and interests. Lacking work experience, a recent graduate can use hobbies and interests to show his personal skills.

Experienced candidates might follow a short introduction with a list of their work experience, in reverse chronological order. The introduction must identify the key strengths of the candidate and sell the remainder of the CV to the reader. The most relevant experience, which is the current or most recent job, appears next. Work history more than about ten years old is less significant, but still needs listing to complete the picture.

STYLE

The CV is a factual, informative report. It does not contain opinion. Facts are most clearly described in short sentences, using simple vocabulary. The CV should be concise. A bullet-point format can be used to convey information briefly, and also allows the author to avoid repeating the word 'I'.

Whenever possible, achievements should be specific and quantified. For example, list exam grades.

Describe activities so that there is no doubt that they are your own achievements and not those of your department.

Verbs like *wrote, trained, tested, arranged, developed* and *commissioned* help to convey an impression of action and achievement.

Your CV should have a positive, optimistic tone. To keep the length down to one or two pages, it has to be written concisely. A punchy style will be suitably brief and hold the reader's attention. CVs should be mildly boastful, but completely accurate. It is useful to check through for self-deprecation.

Look for words such as *small*, *only* and *minor*. These words convey a sense of failure and disappointment. A more positive tone will emerge if they are edited out.

The correct length for a CV depends on the candidate's age and experience. A new graduate might manage on a single page of A4. After five years' work I would recommend two pages. One page is no longer sufficient to describe all your experience. Work experience older than about ten years needs abbreviating. Page two contains this older information, and your qualifications. After ten years' work experience qualifications are less important than experience and may be thus relegated. A CV that is longer than two pages is tedious. After all, the whole idea is to whet the reader's appetite so that you are invited to an interview. It is good to have lots of impressive detail to add at the interview.

Your CV can be tailored to each position applied for. Alternatively, you can produce a single CV, and make sure that the accompanying covering letter is effectively aimed at each particular vacancy. The latter approach is the best policy, because it allows a single perfect CV to be developed. You might think that there is a case for a second CV if applying for two distinct types of work. For example, prepare one CV for sales jobs and a second for production jobs. However, by applying for different types of job, you risk adopting the ineffective shotgun approach.

A CV must never appear mass-produced. Each copy needs to be produced with loving care. Again, I emphasise the importance of a word processor and high-quality printer.

DAVID JONES

10 Homelane   Tel: Home 01783 123456
Hometown   Work 01783 120120
Sussex HT1 2AB

BACKGROUND

I graduated with an upper second in technical design from
the University of Newtown in 1980. I obtained a PhD from
Oldtown in 1990.

I am a chartered design engineer with wide professional
experience. My previous employers include Robinsons, Watts
Petroleum and Combined Pharmaceuticals.

My present job is as a project manager in the maintenance
section at Tinpot Engineering.

CAREER HISTORY

Project Manager, Plant Maintenance Section, Tinpot Engineering, Hometown. 1995–present

- Design and install plant improvements, with responsibility
  for critical path analysis and resource allocation.
- Liaise with contractors and suppliers to install new equipment.
- Control project budgets and authorise payments to suppliers.

**Development Engineer, Combined Pharmaceuticals,
Pasthometown.** 1990–1995

- Supported the plant operating team on a day-to-day basis.
- Liaised with the technical department and helped with the
  modification of equipment.
- Carried out automation of tablet-making equipment, powder
  recovery and product purification plant.
- Debottlenecked packing plant, commissioning computer-
  controlled equipment.

- Liaised with sales and purchasing, travelling to customers' and suppliers' premises.

Senior Designer, Watts Petroleum, Pasthometown.
1985–1990
Plant Design Office
- Prepared detailed designs for schemes to convert oil platforms to remote operation, using computer-aided drawing and writing Pascal programs.
- Liaised with design contractors to prepare detailed design specifications and costings.

Platform Operations Development Section
- Developed a technique to separate salt water from oil at high pressure using a new, computer-controlled membrane process. I obtained an extramural PhD through Oldtown University while doing this work.
- Prepared user and technical specifications, and liaised with a contractor to convert a salt-water separation plant to the membrane process.
- Successfully commissioned the plant on time and with no extra cost.
- Operated test equipment in a production environment.

Design Officer, Watts Petroleum, Wattstown Research Centre. 1984–1985
- Supported the pilot plant development team on a day-to-day basis.
- Tested equipment and designed modifications.

Design Officer, Robinsons Automation, Robinstown.
1980–1984
- Carried out the product development of double-action Suresafe solenoid valves.
- Carried out plant trials at Edinburgh and Bristol production plants.
- Liaised with sales and technical services, monitoring and supporting the use of Suresafe valves worldwide.

EDUCATION AND QUALIFICATIONS

University of Oldtown 1986–1990
PhD in the 'computer control of oil separation plant using membranes'.

Robinstown College of Further Education 1983
A level in Art (C)

University of Newtown 1977–1980
BSc (Hons) upper second in technical design

Queen Elizabeth 1st School, Northend. 1970–1977
GCSEs
Maths (A), Physics (A), Geography (A), Chemistry (B), German (B), Biology (C), English Language (C), History (C)

A levels
Maths (A), Applied Maths (B), Geography (A)

Institution of Design Engineers 1991
I am a chartered design engineer (CEng)

PERSONAL
British; Date of birth 12/9/59; Married;
One child; Excellent health.

Example of a CV for a (fictitious) final-year undergraduate

DAVID JONES

Room A100   Tel: 0133 12345
Ardwick Hall   e-mail: david.jones@newuni.ac.uk.
University of Newtown
Newtown
Sussex NT1 2XY

BACKGROUND

I am a final-year undergraduate studying technical design at the University of Newtown. I expect to graduate with either a first or an upper second, and hope to follow a technical career in plant automation.

EDUCATION AND QUALIFICATIONS
University of Newtown 1977–1980
Final year: BSc (Hons) in technical design

Queen Elizabeth 1st School, Northend. 1970–1977
GCSEs
Maths (A), Physics (A), Geography (A), Chemistry (B), German (B), Biology (C), English Language (C), History (C)

A levels
Maths (A), Applied Maths (B), Geography (A)

EMPLOYMENT HISTORY
Frozen PetFoods Ltd. June–September 1978
- Operated fish-packing equipment on a production line. I worked as a team member on shifts.

Northend Leisure Centre July–September 1977
- Worked as a swimming-pool attendant. I dealt with customers and supervised happy hour children's games and swimming lessons.

Northend Leisure Centre August 1976
- Served in the cafeteria, dealing with customers and preparing hot drinks and snacks.

HOBBIES AND INTERESTS
I am treasurer of the university orienteering club, and have represented the university in orienteering competitions.

PERSONAL
British; Date of birth 12/9/59; Single.

Example of a covering letter for a (fictitious) final-year undergraduate applying for a job as a graduate trainee where teamwork and communication skills are required

> David Jones
> 10 Homelane
> Hometown
> Sussex
> HT1 2AB

12 November 19XX

Dear Mrs Smith

Graduate Trainee Vacancy, Reference JS96/1

I would like to apply for the job of graduate trainee, advertised in the *Daily Chronicle*. I enclose my CV.

May I take this opportunity to draw your attention to the following aspects of my career history?

- treasurer of the university orienteering team
- holiday job working as a team member at Frozen PetFoods Ltd.
- experience of dealing with customers in holiday jobs at Northend Leisure Centre

Yours sincerely
David Jones

Chapter 7

Application Forms

Application forms are particularly popular with employers using the milk round to recruit final-year undergraduates. Most companies have their own application form. University careers offices have a supply of standard application forms for those companies who do not.

Although application forms can be daunting at first, the questions are fairly standard. Once you have completed one, further application forms are easy.

When an employer asks a candidate to fill in an application form it provides a framework for the selection process. The interviewer will refer to it constantly during the interview. Therefore the candidate should keep a record of the completed application form and read it just before the interview so that he knows what is coming next. A useful tip is to photocopy the blank form and fill in the copy in rough. Finally, complete the original with great care.

Employers may insist that candidates complete an application form in order to discourage half-hearted applicants.

Since all candidates complete the same application form, they can be compared equally in deciding which ones to invite to interview. Completing the form seems a chore, but it has to be done with painstaking care. You must follow the instructions and complete the form in your best handwriting. This should normally be in black ink, as the completed form may be photocopied by the employer.

A reader will draw conclusions about the candidate from the way the form is completed. Block letters throughout might be legible but creates a poor impression of literacy. The reader may speculate that the candidate cannot do joined-up writing. There must be no spelling errors or messy smudges.

55

Return application forms promptly, in a white envelope with a first-class stamp. Put the job reference on the envelope. Avoid excessive folding. Optional reply cards to acknowledge the application are sometimes enclosed with the application form. They should be filled in because this gives the impression that you consider the application to be important.

DIFFICULT QUESTIONS

All application forms contain a few difficult questions, though some are more difficult than others. Application forms containing difficult questions are not all bad news: with any luck some of the competition will be put off applying!

All questions must be answered. If a question is clearly not applicable, write 'not applicable'. Do not just ignore it.

The following are some common tricky questions.

Question: Why are you leaving your present job?
Answer: I want more money (*or* I want more experience to develop my career; *or* I want to get on and need more opportunities; *or* I enjoy my current job but am now ready for a new challenge).

Any one of these is an acceptable answer. There are many reasons for leaving a job. Usually there will be a combination of reasons that are too complex to discuss. Employers also do not really expect candidates to tell the whole truth if, for example, they do not get on with their present boss. There are several acceptable explanations for wanting to leave your job, but none for failing to get on with your boss. Choose a good reason for leaving your job and keep the reply brief. Answers to this question are believable in inverse proportion to their length.

Question: What strengths do you bring to this job? (*or* What makes you suitable for this job?)

Answer: (for a job requiring problem-solving skills) I believe that I'm good at analysing situations and identifying what the most important aspects are – in other words getting to the root cause of a problem quickly.

At first this question seems horrendous. However, it is an open question, which a prepared job-searcher thrives on. To use it successfully, keep the reply relevant to the job vacancy. The advert will contain vital clues about what the employer is looking for. Make relevant claims, and be able to back them up with examples.

Sufficient detail is needed to whet the employer's appetite. Probing questions will follow at the interview, provided the application is successful. What are the achievements that will demonstrate the strengths you claim to have? Keep something really special to talk about at the interview.

This question allows the candidate to direct the course of the interview in a positive way. Ideally, the interviewer will discover something good about the candidate.

It is advisable to avoid making too many claims. This will dilute the important messages. It is impossible for someone to be good at everything. Replies should avoid sounding pompous.

Do not be afraid to leave space on the form. That is preferable to spoiling your message by saying too much.

Question: Why do you want to work here?
Answer: I'm interested in working on [whatever they do there].

A good answer to this question shows a knowledge of what the job involves, and also how you feel about it. An unacceptable reply would be: 'I want to leave my present employer [for whatever reason].'

If this question does not appear on the application form then it will do at interview. Eventually you will have to think of an answer.

You should do some research to find out something about the company to use in reply. Your answer must be positive so that any follow-up questions will be positive too. Saying that you want to leave your present employer may provoke a negative question.

Question: What salary do you require?

This is the most unfair question to appear on the application form.

A candidate is less likely to get an interview if he does not answer the question. However, as a negotiating ploy he should not say how much he would like until he is sure the employer wants him.

New graduates should find out what a normal starting salary is, and add 5 per cent.

For candidates making career moves, the best approach is to guess what the salary for the job is and add 5 per cent. It is possible to put down a salary range, but if the range is too high, the candidate does not get an interview, while if it is too low, he will, if successful, be offered less than he might otherwise have been.

Employers will not normally pay more than 10 to 20 per cent above a candidate's current salary.

You must never ask for less than your current salary unless you are currently unemployed. If you do, an employer will be suspicious. He might think that you are desperate to leave your current job for a reason that would also make you unsuitable for this job.

Question: Who is responsible to you in your present job?

Remember that firms have different management styles. If an employer has an organic management structure, you may be managing people for whom you are not the direct line manager. Include people who work for you indirectly, explaining how they are responsible to you. Do not underestimate your importance in your current job.

Question: What are your responsibilities in your present job?

Sometimes people are responsible for things like making presentations, supervising trials, writing reports, speaking to customers, etc. These things are important but their significance is not immediately obvious. For example, speaking to customers is a sign that a candidate is reliable and presentable, and can be trusted to handle the firm's most important relationship.

The interviewer will ask about these things at the interview, so you must have examples of achievements or experiences to support any claims.

Question: Have you any additional information?

Application forms normally invite candidates to add additional information, or to continue on a separate sheet. It is a sign of interest and enthusiasm to do so, but remember that the reader has limited time on each application. Any information must be relevant. It is acceptable to enclose a CV, when invited. A separate list of your strengths relevant to the job is a possibility. Where additional information is more than a few words, it should be typed.

Question: Have you any hobbies?
Answer: I am chairman of the university bridge society.

This is an ideal reply for a final-year undergraduate.

New graduates have little work experience to use in their application. For them, this is an important question. It is also relevant to state any recent interests, such as those at school, if they show teamwork, initiative or responsibility.

Experienced candidates should be cautious when listing hobbies or outside interests. You must balance the desire to show off your strengths against the danger of appearing preoccupied with your hobby. If asked about their hobbies, experienced candidates should list those that are relevant to the job.

Some hobbies clearly suggest the ability to work in a team, to organise things, to show creativity or initiative. However it is hard to see the relevance of hobbies such as train-spotting or stamp-collecting. Think how your interest will be received.

It is good if the interviewer discovers something in common with the candidate to discuss at the interview. Hobbies provide a chance for this to happen, irrespective of whether the hobby is relevant to the job. If your hobby provides a talking point at the interview do not miss this opportunity to sell a key strength pertaining to the job vacancy.

REFERENCES

Application forms nearly always ask for two references.

One reference must be a previous employer. Students can use their course leader, their personal tutor or the head of their academic department.

The second reference may be a family friend, if you prefer. You must read the instructions provided on the form. Some employers require a third reference. If you have changed jobs recently, a new employer might ask for references from all previous employers for the last three years.

Students should speak to their course leader or tutor to confirm that they are willing to provide a reference. Take this opportunity to prime them with details about holiday work, prizes won, or any other strong points that you want to publicise.

If there is something in your background to prevent someone providing a good reference, it is essential that you do not supply their name. People will only give a good reference, or none at all. They are afraid that the candidate will prosecute them or their institution if the employer subsequently rejects him. Should anyone decline to provide a reference when a prospective employer asks, this will raise the alarm.

When working, and planning a career move, the situation is more complex. It will spoil your working relationship if you ask your boss to provide a reference. In these circumstances, ask the new employer not to approach your existing employer before a firm job offer is made. In normal circumstances, any boss will be willing to provide a reference. If your boss likes you he will wish you well in your future career. If he does not like you he will be pleased that you are leaving. It is also possible, though not as satisfactory, to give the name of the company personnel manager. When the time comes, he will either provide the reference or ask around to find someone else who will.

CHECK LIST

I have heard a number of stories, which may or may not be true, claiming that some major employers receive so many application forms that they do a preliminary screening exercise. They reject applications that have any of the following faults:

- smudges, crossings-out and general untidiness
- Tippex
- blank boxes, even if the questions were not applicable
- spelling mistakes
- obvious errors, such as not all parts of the question answered

It makes sense to avoid the above problems, just in case the stories are true.

Check your application form carefully. If you have spoiled it, ask for another.

Chapter 8

Advertisements

Advertisements attract different levels and types of response depending on where they appear. A trade journal might have about 50 replies, each from someone with relevant qualifications and experience. They should all get a fair examination. The CV or application form will be read in detail. On the other hand, an advertisement in a national newspaper such as the *Daily Telegraph* will attract over 400 replies. Most of these will be not quite so relevant to the vacancy. It is vital to enclose a good covering letter stating your main qualifications and experience. The covering letter should focus on the job not the applicant, picking out the key words from the advert.

When replying to an advertisement, you should read it through repeatedly. Analyse the important things the advertisement asks for. Highlight or write down the key words and use them in your covering letter.

Identify achievements that show the strengths asked for in the advertisement.

If an advertisement says that further information is available, follow up this invitation. More information will allow you to direct your effort correctly, by understanding precisely what it is that the job requires. Speaking on the telephone to someone who will interview the applicants requires care. An interviewer, perhaps subconsciously, might screen candidates by phone. You should try to be the one asking the questions and avoid saying too much about yourself. On the other hand, the fact that you have bothered to ask for further information will be remembered. It will be seen as a sign of genuine interest.

SALES JOBS

Advertisements for salespersons may not be what they seem. Many jobs require a special ability to withstand rejection. Telesales jobs are an example. The rejection rates are so enormous that it takes an exceptional type of person to carry on regardless. When an advertisement claims that 'earnings are limited only by your own effort', this implies that it is commission-based. Perhaps it is on commission only. Allowing for the possibility of no sales and no pay, is it really a job at all?

Read the detail of the advertisement. It is a mistake to provide your name and address to a disreputable outfit who might try some high-pressure selling on you. Never follow up an advertisement for a job that involves paying a fee. There are many people who will take advantage of your desperation to find a job.

AGENCY ADVERTISEMENTS

Companies advertise through an agency for two reasons: first, they do not want to make the effort required for a large recruitment exercise, and so leave the first stage of selection to an agency; second, they might not want to be seen to advertise frequently, or people will suspect a high staff turnover.

Many agency advertisements do not mention the company name. Maybe the agency does not want candidates to contact the company directly in case it loses its commission.

Sometimes an agency tests the market with bogus advertisements. It may want to appear to have more clients than it really does. Sometimes a vacancy is withdrawn or filled in the time taken for the advert to come to press. Vague adverts are most likely to be false. Ones containing lots of detail about the location, the job and the employer are more likely to be genuine.

Candidates like to know the name of the employer. When it is a prestigious company, the name alone induces candidates to apply.

Agencies often advertise some top jobs. However, it is probably not a good idea to allow an agency to put your details on file.

When replying to an agency advertisement, you should be prepared for a surprise telephone call either at home or at work. The agency will ask a few questions designed to eliminate some candidates from a long list of applicants. The short list of potential candidates is invited to interview. This screening interview carried out over the telephone is just as important as a face-to-face interview and must be adequately prepared for. It is annoying to be screened out in such a casual manner, especially if you think you could do the job.

To prepare for a 'surprise' telephone call, list your relevant key achievements and main selling points or strengths. Keep the list near the telephone. Have the advertisement handy, preferably with a number of key words highlighted to identify the job requirements.

When an agency telephones it is possible to delay by requesting a few details about the job. Ask for the name of the company and the caller. Say that you have to fetch a pen and paper. You can use this time to collect your prepared material and get ready to sell yourself. Ideally you should be knowledgeable about the company the job is with, and be able to explain how useful and relevant your training and experience are.

NEWSPAPER ADVERTISEMENTS CALENDAR

The major daily newspapers publish job advertisements on specific days. Thursday is the most important day of the week for most types of vacancy. Currently, the days used by each paper for the various kinds of jobs are:

| **Monday** | *Independent* | Networks (Information Technology) |
| | *Guardian* | Marketing and Public Relations, Creative, Media, Sales, Secretarial |

Tuesday	*Guardian*	Education, Lecturing, Teaching
	Independent	Media, Marketing, Sales
	Times	Legal
	Telegraph	General, Engineering, Overseas, Graduates
Wednesday	*Independent*	Accounting, Financial, Legal
	Guardian	Senior, Public Service, Health, Housing, Environment
	Times	La Crème de la Crème (PA)
	Telegraph	Education
Thursday	*Telegraph*	General Management, Engineering, Personnel, Sales
	Independent	Education, Graduates, Public, General
	Guardian	Computing, Graduates
	Times	Managing Directors, La Crème de la Crème
Friday	*Times*	Education

THE INTERNET

The Internet is growing rapidly, and employers already advertise vacancies on it. For graduates, this makes large amounts of information much more accessible.

The Internet attracts students and is widely available to them. It has the potential in the near future to become the main source of careers information for final-year students.

Graduate Opportunities

The *Graduate Opportunities* (*GO*) journal is available from university careers offices. Some of the information is also available on the Internet at web site http://www.get.co.uk.

The hard copy of *GO97* was a more complete source of

information than the Internet in November 1996. However, it is unclear when this issue of the hard copy was released. Students need up-to-date information at the start of term, and the Internet looks like the best way to provide it.

The computer invites final-year students to register their interest in a company using this web site, and promises that someone will send further details by post.

Prospects Finalist

Web site http://www.prospects.csu.man.ac.uk will help the user to do a job search. The user enters information about his subject of study, preferred occupation, type of employer and favoured location. The computer suggests a list of employers. Employer details include the postal address and method of application.

For students already hooked on the Internet, this is an exciting way to do a job search.

Other advertisements on the Internet

It is possible to search for a job on the Internet by reading the web pages of newspapers and journals such as the *New Scientist*, and the *Times Higher Educational Supplement*. Some of them have to be subscribed to, but most are free. The Internet is especially helpful for reading the jobs pages of foreign publications, which are otherwise hard to obtain. This should speed up the brain drain dramatically! To read the advertisements, you need to find the correct web site. Most publications give their web site in each issue. The easy approach is to get a copy and write it down.

Some employers, when advertising in newspapers and journals, give their web site for further details.

In the milk round, employers use their web sites to provide up-to-date information on the venues and dates of their careers fairs and presentations.

Chapter 9

Speculative Approaches

Answering adverts is probably the first method people consider when searching for a job. The advantage of replying to an advert is that a vacancy definitely exists. If time allows, however, other approaches should be considered. You could try writing speculative applications to potential employers; using your personal contacts; or sending your CV to a recruitment agency.

Final-year undergraduates can find out about potential employers at their university careers office. They can then make speculative approaches.

WRITING A LETTER TO A POTENTIAL EMPLOYER

Many companies try to recruit new graduates as a matter of course. Large companies send information to universities. Company brochures are stored in the employer files at university careers centres and students can refer to them to find details of addresses. This is a special case. Final-year undergraduates do not need to see an advert to know that there will be vacancies. They should follow the instructions in the employer information. In this situation employers often prefer an application form to a CV. Enclose a brief covering letter with your form or CV.

Writing to a potential employer is not easy. Uninvited applications require more preparation than applications for advertised vacancies. It has to appear that the candidate has a genuine interest in the company, so much so that he is writing to ask about the possibility of a vacancy. Except in the case of final-year undergraduates, an application comprises a polished

CV and an immaculate handwritten covering letter. The letter explains the particular strengths that the candidate could use in a potential vacancy. However, it must explain this without any clear guidance about what the job requirements are. The candidate should also explain why he has an interest in this particular company.

In theory, any expanding company might need new staff. Lots of other companies, especially big ones, need staff to replace those who leave or retire.

When you write to a company, your details will be kept on file until a suitable vacancy becomes available. Then you will be considered along with other speculative applications. On occasions, companies have so many speculative approaches that they choose not to advertise. In this way you get considered for a vacancy that you would otherwise not have known about.

Writing directly to a firm, with a good covering letter and CV, is evidence that you really want to work especially for them. Employers appreciate it.

Many companies regularly advertise in professional magazines and national newspapers such as the *Daily Telegraph*. Find out who advertises for your sort of job, checking back issues over about 18 months to two years. The person who got that job might have left now, or there might be an additional vacancy.

When writing a speculative application, it is best to find out the name of the company's personnel manager. You could get this either from an old advert or from the firm's switchboard. Phoning the switchboard at a quiet time of day is the best way to find out about the company. Ask who could send you company reports and any product information that might be relevant. Most firms have someone who liaises with local schools, and that person is the one to ask for information.

You might decide to make a speculative telephone call to the personnel manager. Should he say there are no vacancies, then try to keep the door open for the future. However, you might think it too bold to make a speculative approach by phone. It would be more polite, and ultimately more successful, to write in the hope of being invited to attend an interview.

There are some problems with writing on spec to a company.

- *Information problem.* There is less information available about the particular requirements of any vacancy. Therefore it is difficult to know which strengths and achievements to emphasise in your application.

- *Future vacancy problem.* Writing to a potential employer without success may alienate them. They might advertise in the future, and once a decision to reject an applicant has been made it is hard to reverse. Supposing a vacancy arises in six months' time; the personnel manger will know that you have been looking for a job, without success, for more than six months.

USING YOUR CONTACTS

Most people will be pleased to help if they are able. When you have a personal contact who can help it is a good idea to ask. The problem is *when* to approach your contact. Any material that you supply to them, for example your CV, must be perfectly presented. This is a matter of courtesy. Consequently, it is best to wait until you have prepared a polished CV before making contact.

Should a contact provide an opening that looks promising, you must reply promptly. You need to know if the opportunity is a good one, and should therefore test the marketplace before asking a contact for help.

Occasionally, it may transpire that a friend can actually provide a job. However, never depend entirely on a contact. Friends who make promises are sometimes not able to deliver. Continue to pursue other opportunities simultaneously.

Should you let a contact know you are trying to find a job, it is polite to inform them when you accept a position elsewhere.

Thank them for their support and any effort that they have made for you.

SENDING YOUR CV TO A RECRUITMENT AGENCY

In the job market there are two types of agency: one acts for the employee and the other for the company. The employee's agency is called an outplacement agency and the company's a recruitment agency. The outplacement agency searches for a job to suit their candidate. The recruitment agency advertises vacancies and looks for candidates. Since the two jobs are complementary, and the agencies work in the same job market, there are opportunities for collusion.

The arrangement is like a dating agency, except that in a dating agency the same agent works for both sides. Employers send in their job specifications and employees send in their CVs. In the middle someone tries to fix them up with a suitable match.

Always remember that agencies are in the job market for a living, so you cannot expect free help. You pay an outplacement agency's fee, normally a fraction of your first year's salary. A recruitment agency is paid by, and acts for, an employer, but has unusual power over the candidate: while it cannot offer him a job, it can prevent him from being considered for one.

Here are some problems with applying for a job through a recruitment agency:

• *Salary problem.* Normally, a recruitment agency will give guidelines on the salary for the job. This is often in the advert, and always in the job specification sent to potential candidates. However, it is in the agency's best interests to offer a high salary so that a large number of good candidates apply. This may lead to a mismatch between what the candidate expects and what the employer is actually prepared to pay.

You can avoid having to accept a lower-than-expected salary

by never accepting a verbal offer. Wait for the written offer before altering any job search plans.

• *Familiarity problem*. Once a recruitment agency has your CV they will remember you when any future vacancies arise. This can work against you if the agency holds a poor first impression.

You can get round this problem if you can guess the identity of the employer behind the advert and write to them directly. This requires a good knowledge of the job market. A serious job-seeker may develop that knowledge.

You might discover the company's name by looking back through the last three to six months of the advertisement press. Notice the names of companies advertising similar jobs. Often if a company is unsuccessful in a round of advertising they re-advertise through an agency. This is to cut back on effort, and to avoid appearing to have a recruitment problem.

Most companies stick to the same recruitment agency, sometimes using the company name and sometimes advertising anonymously. Agencies often use the same publications to advertise in. The location of the appointment is generally given in the advert so that candidates can decide before applying if they are interested in working in that area. These clues help to identify the company behind the advert.

• *Company name*. When an agency advertises a vacancy, the name of the company is normally withheld. This is to prevent people applying directly to the employer. If candidates introduce themselves directly, the agency might not get its commission. It also misses its chance to reject candidates and so loses control over whom the employer interviews. Once an agency has a candidate's CV, and so can justifiably claim that it introduced the candidate, it will sometimes reveal who the employer is.

Candidates are expected to list the companies to whom they do not want their details forwarded. This prevents current working relationships from being spoiled by the discovery that an employee is looking for a new job.

COMPETITION FOR VACANCIES

In a job search, most people reply to advertisements. Vacancies definitely exist, but a lot of other people are competing for them. Speculative applications are the other way round. It would be unwise to put too much store by speculative approaches because you cannot be sure that the opportunities exist. However, if they do exist, fewer people will be competing for them.

A follow-up letter is almost always worthwhile.

Example of a covering letter for a (fictitious) final-year undergraduate to make a speculative application to a potential employer

David Jones
10 Homelane
Hometown
Sussex
HT1 2AB

12 November 19XX

Dear Sir or Madam

Graduate Technical Design Vacancies

I am a final-year undergraduate studying technical design at the University of Newtown. I hope to graduate with an upper second. I am interested in working in the petrochemical industry, and I am especially interested in technical support work. Do you have any vacancies at Watts Petroleum? I enclose my CV.

May I draw your attention to the following points from my CV?

- treasurer of the university orienteering team
- holiday job working as team member at Frozen Petfoods Ltd
- experience of dealing with customers in holiday jobs at Northend Leisure Centre

Yours faithfully
David Jones

Chapter 10

The Milk Round

The annual milk round of British universities is a recruitment exercise that targets final-year undergraduates. Each October major employers tour the universities searching for the best people who will graduate that academic year. Their quest begins in October and November with careers fairs, continues with interviews at universities, and ends with second-round interviews at assessment centres. By the end of February, lucky undergraduates have secure job offers, which are normally not conditional on their class of degree. Employers go away content that they have secured the best possible people.

The milk round is a remarkable recruitment exercise because of the large number of jobs involved. It is special because for most recruits these will be their first real jobs.

THE TIMETABLE

The milk-round timetable varies between universities and between the different employers. Variations are inevitable because all employers cannot go to all universities simultaneously. Participating employers usually visit about six universities each. However, students from universities not visited can still participate.

You should visit your university careers centre at the very beginning of the first term of your final year. Find the notice boards where jobs and events are advertised. Look for the various free publications. Careers centres have all sorts of literature about different careers. The main thing is to find out about the timetable of events. All universities organise a series of talks on completing your CV, attending interviews, etc. Later there are careers fairs and company presentations. Finally, you need to be aware of the closing dates for applications to companies interviewing on the milk round. Sometimes this information is not readily available, and you will need to make regular visits to the careers centre throughout October in order to keep ahead of events.

A typical milk-round timetable is as follows:

September and October: Visit the careers office weekly. Do not expect anyone to tell you about things. You will have to find things out for yourself. Firm up on ideas about the type of career and companies you are interested in. Write your CV. Ask for a standard application form and think about how to complete it. Make a note of important events such as careers fairs. Look out for those firms with early closing dates for milk-round applications. The beginning of term is academically quiet, so make as much progress now as is possible.

November and December: Submit companies' own application forms. Sometimes these may be returned to the careers office; otherwise post them directly. Do not restrict yourself to those companies advertising vacancies. Apply directly to all the companies you would like to work for. Visit the careers fairs, asking as many questions as possible.

Some milk-round interviews take place in November and December; the closing date for applications to many other companies will be around this time too.

January and February: Most milk-round first interviews take place on campus.

February and possibly March: Second interviews are held at company assessment centres. These are often two-day events.

March: Consider suspending your job-search activities. Although there is no time limit for applications, the milk round is over.

File company addresses and careers literature away until after the exams. You need to get the best class of degree you can. The Easter holidays are for serious revision.

April to June: Work hard for exams.

July: Resume the job search.

UNIVERSITY CAREERS CENTRES

Your university careers centre is the first place to go in your milk-round job search. If there is another university nearby, visit their careers centre too. If they are a more established university they are more likely to have companies visiting on the milk round. Careers centres are often busy, with just a handful of staff to service thousands of students. Do not expect too much personal service. A short chat with a careers adviser is possible, but you may need to book it in advance; advisers usually become fully booked by the end of October. Alternatively, computer packages are available for students to experiment with. The Internet contains at least one job-search package (see p.66).

Careers centres have rows of employer files. This is because all companies that want to recruit new graduates write to the careers centres, who then open files on them. These employer files are likely to contain a glossy brochure and a company application form. The brochure will supply the address to reply to. Read the instructions carefully. Alternatively, companies interviewing on the milk round will collect application forms from the careers centre, saving students the postage.

Many students fail to make proper use of their careers centre. Staff say that undergraduates expect to be spoon-fed, an impossible task given the student:staff ratio. It is up to you to stay in touch. Each week, you should collect the vacancies bulletins and read the notice boards. Ask staff for the dates of careers fairs and company presentations, and the closing dates for milk-round applications.

CAREERS FAIRS

In October and November, often on Wednesdays, companies hold careers fairs, where they set out stalls to attract students. The fairs may be held in the student union building or a sports hall. Typically, 30 to 50 companies each set up an advertising display. Two or three graduate employees accompany the company's graduate recruitment officer. Each display has a stock of glossy brochures and a supply of application forms. The staff chat with visiting students to provide basic information. They can explain what the company does, how many vacancies they have, and which degree disciplines they want. Since many staff at the fair are recent graduates, they can give first-hand accounts of their company's training programme.

The fairs aim to advertise the company names and to inform undergraduates of the choices available to them. They are excellent opportunities for students to find out about careers with the participating companies. Ask lots of questions, and let the representative of the company tell you all about it.

Students visiting the fairs can also ask about the qualities that employers are looking for. This research will help you to complete your application form and impress at the interview. An employer wants to know that you are especially interested in his particular company.

Some companies at the fairs are looking for hundreds of recruits; others for only four or five.

Some companies plan to interview at the university on the milk round. Others invite students to send completed application forms to their assessment centres. The address is usually on the back of the application form or in the glossy brochure.

WHAT ARE COMPANIES LOOKING FOR ON THE MILK ROUND?

In general, companies are not looking for a particular degree discipline, a particular degree classification, A-level points or a particular university. These things are properties of the system and not of the individual. Qualifications enable a candidate to apply but they are not decisive in getting selected. All the facts about a candidate will be considered. The most important information is also the most subjective. Communication and interpersonal skills are what employers want first and foremost. They also look for evidence of initiative and energy. Work experience in a year out and vacation jobs are disproportionately useful for showing these attributes.

Students who are studying really useful subjects cannot expect to walk into a job just because their course is relevant. Similarly, those who emerge from less stretching courses need not worry that they will be unduly disadvantaged. Of course, students doing economics will have an advantage when applying to the high-street stores, for example. But when the all-important personal qualities are taken into account, how people used their vacation time is more important than the subjects they studied.

Academic life revolves around the degree classification. A first-class honours degree is a lifelong asset, if only because it bolsters self-confidence. People sell themselves on the strength of a first-class degree years after it has ceased to have any relevance, and not just during a job search. On the milk round, the degree classification that you expect has a limited value as a selling point. However, milk-round candidates need to be certain of at least a lower second, and should support their claims using second-year results. In general, milk-round recruiters pass over candidates who expect to get a third-class honours or a pass degree. Job offers are usually made unconditional upon the degree classification obtained. Employers are confident that they are selecting the right candidates. The right candidates are not the sort of people who might fail their degrees.

Exceptionally, milk-round employers have an A-level points cutoff of 22 points, below which they will not recruit. The points system is as follows:

Grade A = 10 points
Grade B = 8 points

Grade C = 6 points
Grade D = 4 points
Grade E = 2 points
Grades at A/S level count for half points.

The advantage of using A-level grades is that candidates already know their results. It is, however, unfair to those candidates who for some reason underperformed in their A levels. For example, some students benefit from a public-school education while others attend inner-city comprehensives. Poor A levels can be accounted for by parents moving home at a critical stage, or by family upsets coinciding with exam preparation. If you got fewer than 22 A-level points, be prepared to explain why. Usually, employers are sympathetic, especially if you now expect a good degree.

Students are sometimes anxious that employers will not want them because of the university they attend. Your university is frequently irrelevant. The employer is interested in you, not your place of learning. However, it is undeniable that there is a shortage of companies conducting milk-round interviews at less well-established universities. This is not because employers do not want students from these places, merely that traditionally they have visited other universities and need a good reason to change their venue. Since it is logistically impossible for all companies to visit all universities, some companies go to certain universities and others visit other ones. No company can afford to alienate students from the universities it does not visit. Therefore, if you are interested in a company which has not visited your university send an application form to head office or the company's recruitment centre. You may then attend a milk-round interview at a nearby university or at the company's assessment centre. The milk-round is like a giant melting pot into which all final-year undergraduates and all companies are thrown. No student should enter it with an inferiority complex due to the university he attends.

Work experience is a key issue for final-year undergraduates. For most it is a problem because not many students have ever had a real job. On the other hand, nearly every final-year undergraduate will have had at least one holiday job. How you describe your holiday job is absolutely vital.

Employers try to interpret the way in which students acquire their holiday jobs. Some find their own jobs; some work for the family firm; others have no job at all. It is good to show initiative by finding your own holiday job. It is a sign that you will show initiative in your future career. It does not matter if the job was for only a week if you found it yourself.

Employers also look for evidence of customer contact. Talking to customers means that you have to use communication skills and interact with others. This experience is extremely valuable. It means that a job as a waitress or shop assistant is really much more significant than you might at first expect.

Those undergraduates who took a year out have more to talk about. Why did they take a year out, and what did they do in it? How much of what they did was their own effort and how much was done for them?

The best way to take a year out is as a sandwich year between the second and final years of your course. This can form a part of the course for which you get a certificate of industrial training. The experience also enhances your understanding of the course. Sandwich courses are available in business studies, engineering, languages and other vocational subjects. The year out gives you the chance to see if your chosen profession is really what you want to do.

Sandwich placement jobs can turn into permanent jobs on graduation. Some companies recruit as many sandwich trainees as possible. They use the sandwich year to assess trainees properly, a sort of extended interview. However, there is no guarantee of a vacancy. A trainee can also use the year to make up his mind about the company. He might form a favourable impression but decide that he does not want to work there.

Responsibility in a club or society is also something employers look for. Being the chairperson or treasurer of a society is a sign of good interpersonal skills and initiative. Such experience is especially valuable if you are involved in setting up a club and take an active part in its organisation. Any team membership, such as the university football or rugby clubs, is welcome. All these things show good communication skills.

COMPLETING APPLICATION FORMS FOR MILK-ROUND JOBS

Milk-round employers typically expect a thousand application forms. They will interview 150 candidates and take 20 recruits. To the student it may seem like a numbers game, but it is not. Each application form you complete needs to stand out from the crowd to have a chance of selection. You need to convince the employer that you really want the job. You must avoid giving the impression that this is just one of the hundreds of jobs you are trying for.

Students' attitudes to completing application forms are often far too casual. Like the whole job-search process, there is no point in making a half-hearted approach. It will not get you anywhere.

Employers are not queuing to give you a job. Most big companies are flexible about how many graduates they recruit each year, depending on how many good candidates they find. You have to prove that you are genuinely interested in doing the job.

The first bit of advice is to complete the application form neatly and tidily. Do not fold the completed form unnecessarily or allow it to become grubby. If your handwriting is illegible, an employer will not pause to decipher it. Should you make a mess of the application form, get a fresh one from the careers office or write to the company for a replacement. Do not bother sending in an application form that is covered in Tippex or crossings-out.

Read the questions properly. Some students are in the habit of rushing and reading only the first part of the question. For example, consider the question: 'Describe an occasion where you took control in a crisis, explaining what you did, and what the outcome was.' The latter two-thirds of this question is often ignored, an oversight that will not impress an employer.

81

Selection may be primarily based on communication skills and personality, qualities that are best assessed at interview. The purpose of the application form is to get an interview in the first place. Remember that the application form sets the agenda for the interview. Some forms specifically ask if there is anything you want to mention at the interview.

Whenever possible, return the form before the milk-round deadline. Those candidates whose forms arrive late have to attend first interviews at assessment centres. Late applicants have a reduced chance of success because some vacancies will already have been allocated. The early bird catches the worm.

PART THREE
THE INTERVIEW

Chapter 11

Interview Preparation

The way to get the job is to prepare for the interview. The way other candidates get rejected is by not preparing. Most of the candidates who progress as far as an interview could do the job. Only those who have prepared for the interview are likely to succeed. Fortunately for you, very few people plan effectively. Most candidates' only preparation is the practice they have had in unsuccessful interviews. For some, the experience of repeated failure has a strongly demoralising effect. Any candidate who wants to can get ahead by making the effort to prepare.

Here is a check list of the things that are needed in preparing for an interview:

- Memorising your achievements.
- Identifying the things you have done in your current job, and the result of each achievement.
- Memorising your CV. The interviewer will refer to it, and so you must remember what it says.
- Reading the advert carefully and identifying the qualities required.
- Choosing the right achievements to talk about for the particular job vacancy.
- Deciding on the best way to talk about your chosen achievements.
- Identifying your strengths and skills, and knowing why you want this job.
- Researching the company with the vacancy.
- Thinking about how to show off your knowledge of the company.
- Knowing how to say you want to work for the company.

- Preparing a career history. Rehearse it to use as a reply to a question at the start of the interview.
- Preparing answers to questions that will come up.
- Preparing travel arrangements.
- Building up self-esteem in the run-up to the interview.
- Immaculate grooming on the day.
- Arriving on time.
- Creating a good first impression.

Memorising your achievements

Chapter 6, Writing a CV, describes how to write down your main achievements. Now is the time to review these achievements in the light of the job in question. You must also memorise your achievements so that you can easily recall them as the need arises in the interview. More detail is necessary. At an interview, you must be able to answer probing questions about the detail of your CV.

In an interview you will need to refer to your achievements without being prompted. That means having the list committed to memory, ready to pull out an appropriate achievement for each question the interviewer asks. Imagine that you have recently designed a new electronic circuit for a burglar alarm system. The interviewer will not ask: 'Tell me about your marvellous design of a circuit for a burglar alarm.' He may not even know that you designed one. However, he will ask open questions like 'What sort of thing did you do at company X?' This allows you to tell him in detail about your circuit.

Identifying the things you have done in your current job

Identify the things you have done personally, and the outcome of each. Avoid talking about the activities of your department because the interviewer will notice. He will wonder if you ever made a contribution yourself or whether you were just carried along by events.

The interviewer is interested in what you can do for him. What you have achieved in your current job is the best indication. It is no good talking about the activities of the department because it is you, not your colleagues, who is applying for the job.

The only situation where the department's activities need to be described is when you explain how you worked effectively within the team. You need to describe how you contributed to the team effort.

Memorising your CV

The interviewer reads your CV before, during and possibly after the interview. Therefore you too must read it just before the interview. Your CV will be used as an agenda, and it must not be a hidden agenda. There will be no opportunity for you to read it during the interview, and so it is important that you memorise it.

You must be able to recall everything you claimed in your CV, and talk about the individual achievements outlined in it.

Reading the advert carefully

When you prepared your covering letter, you identified the key words in the advert describing the qualities required for the job. You must now memorise them for the interview. Just as it was a good idea to repeat the exact words in the covering letter, it is also a good idea to repeat them at the interview. It seems an unsubtle trick, but the interviewer will not notice. The impression created is simply that you are the right person for the job.

Read the advert again carefully. Are there any obvious questions that the interviewer will ask? Are there any other qualities that the employer might want? Read between the lines to infer the other qualities that may be required.

Choosing the right achievements to talk about

You have to talk about your work experience to show that you can do the job and that you are the sort of person to fit in at the company. Decisions made about you will be subjective, because all decisions about people are subjective, and thus the achievements themselves are unimportant. It is the impression they create that matters.

The questions the interviewer asks may not be the precise ones you would like. However, you have to get your strengths and achievements across anyway. The best way to do this is to memorise the three or four main achievements or selling points you need to describe. Hold them in readiness to recount at a suitable opportunity. Prepare your career history, which you hope to deliver early in the interview, so that it encourages the interviewer to ask questions about your main achievements. Get your selling points over steadily throughout the interview, one at a time to avoid confusion. Go over a mental check list towards the end of the interview and make sure that all your strengths have been explained. Do not do this too near the end, or there will be insufficient time remaining to cover any outstanding points.

The interviewer cannot ask direct questions about some of the things you need to talk about. In Chapter 1, we looked at what you need to tell the interviewer to persuade him or her to choose you from among the other candidates. You need to imply that you will get on well with the other people at the company. You need to convince the interviewer that you will work hard. Finally, you should confirm that you really do want the job.

What do you *not* want to talk about?

It would be unwise to mention any arguments you may have had with your boss. No matter how right you were, the interviewer will see things from the boss's point of view. You should avoid criticising your boss or your company. The interviewer will worry that you might say the same about him and his company.

Do not describe any projects that have gone badly wrong or any mistakes that you have made at work. It may be tricky explaining why they were not your fault. No matter how genuine, explanations always seem contrived. The purpose of this exercise is to think ahead to the things that the interviewer currently knows nothing about. Avoid raising the problem questions yourself.

Some interviewers ask nasty questions anyway. They might say: 'Tell me about a job that went wrong.' Or they could ask: 'If you had the chance to do things again what would you do differently?' You should not reply too honestly. You may pick something trivial to use in reply, and need not reveal any dark secrets.

It is unpleasant to talk about why you are unemployed or why you want to leave your present employer, but the interviewer will probably want to know. Since these are negative questions, you should think about how to answer them in a way that sounds positive, and that will avoid further negative questions.

Deciding on the best way to talk about your chosen achievements

How can achievements be described to maximum effect? One technique is to be clear about which selling point is shown by which achievement. Mention only one achievement in reply to each question, giving the interviewer time to digest the information. You should aim to talk in chunks of between twenty seconds and two minutes, the length of your answer depending on how open the question is. You must never ramble on or be irrelevant.

When asked a question, you must answer it, but you can then go on to give more information. A good interviewer will ask an early open question, and follow it up with additional probing questions to elicit more information. A good candidate will detect when more is expected and use the opportunity. The following are examples of open questions that allow a candidate to describe a main achievement:

- What was your best/most exciting/most enjoyable job?
- What is your main strength relevant to this job?
- Tell me about your job.
- Tell me about company X.

- Why do you want to work here?
- What made you apply for this job?

Open questions are the best ones for the candidate to decide for himself what to talk about. A reply to an open question should last between one and two minutes and concentrate on one key selling point. It must be described clearly enough for it to be remembered. Each reply should lead the interviewer to ask another positive question.

Following an open question the interviewer often asks a series of probing questions. Probing questions are a kind of open question, and give the candidate the same chance to sell himself. However, probing questions are normally asked to confirm an impression that the interviewer is already forming. The candidate needs to work out whether it is likely to be a good or a bad impression. If it is a good impression, the probing questions seem friendly and answering them is easy.

Probing questions to confirm good impressions are ones such as:

- So you enjoyed your work at company X?
- How/Why did you do that?
- Tell me more about that.

The candidate can continue to confirm the positive message. He should avoid changing the message or becoming overelaborate, and should not introduce a further selling point or a new achievement in a hurry. The interviewer will need time to understand and remember what the candidate has said.

At the conclusion of a series of positive probing questions the interviewer will sum up his or her positive impression before moving on to something new.

Probing questions to confirm an interviewer's bad impression are ones such as:

- So you didn't like working at X?
- So you could not do the job at X?
- So that was difficult for you?

These questions are a kind of death knell. The interviewer is inviting the candidate to confirm that in some respect he might not be the person for this job. This is a no-win situation for the poor candidate. He might just escape if he recognises what has happened and issues a flat refusal: just say 'No!' If this is an unsuitable reply, try 'That is not true.' In this situation the candidate needs to be prepared for, and unafraid of, a long silence. In interviews it is common for long silences to follow short answers because the interviewer is thinking of the next question. Look the interviewer in the eye, while maintaining a neutral expression. Let it sink in that the interviewer has got it wrong. Never, ever try to explain your way out of a negatively probing question. It only encourages more questions of the same kind. You must stop this line of enquiry with a prompt and firm denial.

You can look at a negatively probing question as an opportunity to show your assertiveness. The interviewer is attempting to deny you the right to this job. You must stand up to the interviewer without becoming aggressive.

You should practise talking about your main achievements, anticipating the probing questions that could arise and how to deal with them.

Identifying your strengths and skills, and knowing why you want this job

The question 'Why do you want this job?' sometimes appears on application forms. It is also an easy, popular and natural question for the interviewer. Yet it is one of those most feared by the interviewee. Candidates fear that the interviewer will find out that they have not bothered preparing a reply, and will form the impression that they do not want the job.

One good reason for wanting a particular job with a particular company is to apply your experience and training to achieve something worthwhile. It is natural to want to achieve exciting things. There is no need to be modest about saying so!

This part of the interview preparation requires you to reason out what is special about your contribution and decide how to put that into words. The explanation must sound genuine. It must be convincing without being too boastful. Tape-recording answers and playing them back is especially helpful for gauging how enthusiastic you can be before starting to sound unbelievable.

Link this into the list of personal strengths you believe you have. Hope for a positive probing question that allows you to describe one.

Researching the company with the vacancy

The first source of information about the company is the job advert. Normally it is possible to follow that up with some genuine research. In the UK all public companies prepare an annual report that acts as a sales document for the shareholders. Annual reports are available at the library or directly from the company. Phone the switchboard and ask if there is someone who could send the report to you. The annual accounts can also be helpful because they tell you if the company makes a profit or a loss. However, some companies make an effort to conceal their true profitability because it is useful information to competitors. They can conceal it by grouping divisions, or by holding a company as a subsidiary. If a company is a wholly owned subsidiary, the figures may be misleading.

If the job is one in which something is made, find out about the manufacturing process. Discover who else makes the same products, who the main customers are, etc. What features does the company sells its products on? How long has the company existed, and have its products or services always been the same?

At an interview you need this information to make the correct passing comments in conversation. You need to avoid saying the wrong things, too. Learn any jargon that is used by the company. Company employees expect newcomers to understand it. If you do not understand essential words or phrases you risk problems at the interview. For example, if applying for a job with British Petroleum, candidates ought to know that LPG stands for liquefied petroleum gas. Anyone who does not know that will be judged to have not read much about BP. Therefore, they are not interested in BP. Rightly or wrongly, people make subjective decisions about candidates.

Trade journals provide an excellent source of information about companies and areas of business. New products appear in advertisement features. Articles discuss the latest technology and equipment. Safety and environmental concerns are considered. Sometimes sensitive issues are mentioned. For example, it would be useful to know that a recent accident had killed someone at the company. This would prompt an interviewee to question the health and safety within this firm. However, it would not be something to ask about at interview if the candidate wanted the job. On the other hand, a new product advertised in the press might be the very reason for the new vacancy. Showing some prior knowledge about the product would be impressive.

How to show off your knowledge of the company

A candidate has to let the interviewer know that he has found out about the company in a discreet way. It will come over in the way he talks, in the small things that are mentioned, and in passing comments. Only one or two bits of information about the company are necessary; more than that spoils the effect, and the deliberate display of knowledge could be irritating.

Interviewers expect candidates to know something about the company, but that is not one of the candidate's selling points. It is something that is taken for granted. However, not knowing anything about the company is sufficient reason for rejection.

One subtle way of showing knowledge of the company would be to ask about a significant product mentioned in the annual report. This reveals that the candidate knows about the product without saying how much or how little, nor where from.

Look out for test questions such as:

- Do you know what we make here?
- Have you heard of product X?
- Did you know that we have a factory in Japan?

Sometimes these questions are phrased in a way that invites a 'no' response. The candidate must say 'Yes', and add some further information if possible. He must resist the temptation to admit ignorance.

The job interview is also a chance for the candidate to decide if he wants the job or not. A candidate who has some information about the company before the interview knows what questions to ask to find out if it is a good place to work.

Interestingly, the candidate, like the interviewer, has to use indirect questioning to find things out. For example, imagine that there has been an accident in which an employee was killed. A candidate should not ask: 'This accident that killed someone: is that why there is a vacancy then?' Instead he should enquire informally, perhaps at lunch: 'Tell me about the safety record here.'

Sometimes the successful interviewee is offered the job on the spot or by telephone later in the day. He might have to reply there and then. When that happens, it is too late to ask for information. He must find out about the company before the interview.

How to say you want to work for the company

Your display of knowledge about the company, its objectives and its markets is one way to convince the interviewer that you want to work there.

You need to show that you understand the way things are done. You must be *au fait* with the technology and procedures the company use.

You must also convince the interviewer that you could do the job. If you cannot show that you have done a similar job before, you have to be enthusiastic about learning how to do the job.

Is there any other way that you can rationalise your desire to work for this company? Maybe a relative works there? Perhaps the locality is especially attractive to you?

It is unlikely that you will be asked all the direct questions you need. You must be prepared to get your reasons across at any time, and not just in reply to specific questions.

Preparing a career history

The initial few exchanges of an interview are often trivial questions such as:

- How did your journey go?
- Did you find your way here all right?

Soon afterwards, when the interviewer hopes that the candidate has settled in, he will ask a more serious question. This is frequently something like:

- Tell me about yourself.
- Tell me about your current job/last job.
- I have read your CV; now would you just summarise your career history again for me?

Sometimes an interviewer will ask a different question. You should reply briefly, and wait for an open question. It is important that you have prepared something to say. You should describe your career history, touching on your major achievements. It is a good idea to deliver your career history as early as possible in the interview.

By reciting your career history, you set an agenda for the remainder of the interview. The advantage of this for the interviewer is that he now has a useful summary of your strengths. Your statement of your career history is like the executive summary of a long report: the listener immediately knows why he should pay attention to what follows. This makes the interviewer's job, which is to absorb and understand information, easier.

Naturally, your introductory career history mentions your main strengths, but not in detail. Hopefully the interviewer will make a note of the things he wants to know more about.

Remember, you must limit the time you spend on any one question to at most two minutes. Longer replies leave the interviewer thinking that you ramble on too much. Too short a reply, perhaps less than a minute, may embarrass the interviewer who might not have had time to prepare his next question! You should practise your introductory career history using a clock and be confident that it takes just under two minutes. The statement should be remembered in near parrot fashion, but it has to be performed spontaneously. You must sound lively, capable and genuine.

Above all, your career history must sound positive. A useful tip is to write it down in longhand, because only then do the little negatives show up. Get rid of any of these that the listener could pick up on. Negatives invite negative probing questions that could end your chances of getting the job. The interviewer must keep thinking 'Yes.'

Your account of your career history comes at a time in the interview when the interviewer is vulnerable, or prone to jump to conclusions. Decisions about people are made very early, and the interviewer subsequently asks questions that seek to reinforce his first impression. Being human, he usually makes an early subjective judgement and then searches for justification. By having the early part of your interview well prepared you will be taking advantage of his human nature.

An interviewer who has formed a good early impression can change his mind if the interview starts to go badly. Contrarily, it is very hard to alter a poor first impression. A well-prepared career history is a prerequisite to getting the job, but it is not sufficient to get it.

Some good ideas for phrases to appear in your career history are:

- I enjoy my work
- My work is very challenging
- I did some interesting work
- I found the job exciting

You may feel that words like 'interesting', 'challenging' and 'exciting' are over the top, but they are not. These words convey a sense of enthusiasm for your work. This is what the interviewer wants and what the candidate has to provide.

If the interviewer asks why you are so enthusiastic, it provides you with the chance to describe a selling point or achievement. Naturally, you want to describe all your main achievements because you are proud of them. When asked about achievements, you should explain them deliberately, clearly and one at a time.

As you recite your introductory career history, you need to say how you feel about the things you have done at work. The interviewer also wants to know this. Why did you do the job? Was it a challenge? Was the outcome good or bad? He wants to know about your feelings to decide what sort of person you are.

Preparing answers to questions that will come up

When he recites his career history, the candidate is hoping to suggest questions to the interviewer. To an extent, some questions are under the control of the candidate. Others arise regardless of his efforts. Interviewers often ask the following:

- Why did you choose the career that you have embarked on?
- What do you see yourself doing in five years' time?

These predictable questions, and others like them, are discussed in Chapter 13.

Candidates are sometimes afraid of certain questions. Interview preparation involves thinking of answers to these questions, and perhaps writing them down for future reference. In preparing answers to interview questions, candidates should guard against replies that lead to negative probing.

Preparing travel arrangements

There is a saying that if you arrive five minutes early for a job interview then you are late! Aim to announce yourself about ten to fifteen minutes ahead of time. Allow enough time to park, straighten clothing and use the toilet. Perhaps use some time before the interview to find out what you can. Work on the first impression that you make on all the other company employees you meet. These people might later be asked what they thought of you.

If travelling by car, allow time for any delays. Journeys through built-up areas in rush hour take longer. Check for roadworks. The Teletext and Ceefax services are often helpful. Prepare the car for its journey. Fill the screen-washer bottle and check the spare tyre. Pack a tool kit and include some old clothes and gloves! Put a road map in the car, even if the route is familiar. Plan the journey so that there is no need to speed.

If things go well and there are no traffic problems, arriving an hour or two early is not a problem. Identify in advance a place near your destination that is suitable for a rest. Try to observe the people coming and going to and from the company, while remaining discreetly unnoticed. This observation can reveal some unexpected, and valuable, information. Avoid practising interview questions so close to the event. Just before an interview, it is important to relax and start taking things in.

It is best to wear a set of travel clothes and change just before the interview. This is particularly important where long journeys are involved, and for journeys involving meals away from home. On the return journey, changing back into your travel clothes keeps the interview suit in top condition for the next interview.

When travelling by train, it is unwise to take the last scheduled train to arrive before the interview. Arriving on time is your responsibility and yours alone. Also, check the time of the last train of the day to return home. Sometimes it is necessary to let the interviewer know when the last train leaves. Before the interview, arrange for a taxi to return to the station. If you are travelling by train, you may have more trouble keeping your clothes in good condition, especially if it rains. It is possible to carry a travel bag containing interview clothes, but this can be cumbersome and seem unusual if observed. Generally, to maintain your composure and make the most favourable impression at an interview, it is better to travel by car.

Building up self-esteem

Chapter 3 describes the importance of self-esteem in performing well at an interview. Part of the preparation for an interview is to time the natural cycle of self-esteem so that it is at a high point on the day. With the other preparations complete, there should be opportunity for relaxation leading up to the interview which should help self-esteem to rise. Playing your favourite music on the car stereo is a good idea. Keep thinking positively, banish thoughts of difficulty, and make a mental image of success. The candidate who has prepared best and left nothing to chance is the one who will succeed.

Immaculate grooming on the day

There is definitely an interview uniform, and it must be in immaculate condition.

For men, the safest outfit consists of a conservative, faintly striped dark-blue or grey suit with a neat shirt and tie. Blue or grey sports jackets and grey trousers are an acceptable alternative. Jeans and cords are not acceptable. You should not wear a plain white shirt, but a conservatively striped one. Black shoes, highly polished for the occasion, are essential. Never wear a pullover, particularly not a sleeveless one. If the weather is very cold, wear a vest with short sleeves so that it is not noticeable. Besides considerations of appearance, it could be warm in the interview room, and you might want to take off your jacket. As a rule at interviews, however, you should not remove your jacket, no matter how uncomfortable you feel! To do so is a sign of excessive familiarity. If you must take it off, at least ask first, or preferably wait for the interviewer to invite you to do so.

Women should look both feminine and professional. A suit consisting of matching jacket and skirt is the safest option, though the interview uniform for women is not as hidebound as that for men. One possible interview outfit might consist of a blouse with a collar, and a skirt on or below the knee. A conventional jacket is essential. If in doubt, err on the side of conventionality rather than fashion. There is no need to be trendy. Wear sensible shoes, preferably black ones.

Women should think of the female employees they might meet at the interview. Other women will remember every detail of your appearance. A moderate amount of make-up and the minimum of jewellery is normal. Excessive perfume could put people off.

The interviewers may have created a mental image of you from your application form or CV. They will modify this image when they see you enter the room. A candidate who appears suitably dressed and immaculately groomed is more likely to make a good impression. The interviewer expects him to be suitable. This good start to the interview influences the type of questions that are asked. Consequently, suitable dress improves the chance of interview success.

Grooming includes many features of appearance. Some of these are not obvious. As well as the way you are dressed, people will notice your physical make-up. How slim are you? Do you look healthy and fit? Are you physically strong? When you speak they will notice your accent. Do you speak clearly, and what is your tone of voice? Do you suffer from any unfortunate mannerisms? Having already considered clothing, what else needs attention?

What about hair? For certain jobs, men may find that tidy, short, but not too short, haircut is important. Men with shoulder-length hair have forgotten or never knew that middle-class people, who are likely to be doing the interviewing, regard long hair with suspicion. The same applies to beards. Perhaps surprisingly, interviewees with beards are discriminated against. Beards are strictly forbidden in jobs where hygiene is important, and in jobs where you might need to wear breathing apparatus. You should not be too proud to have a haircut or shave off your beard. You owe it to yourself to show that you are serious about your job search.

For final-year undergraduates, your first job interview may be the time to change your student image, or at least to tone it down. Men need to shave properly. DIY car mechanics must make sure their fingernails are clean.

Body language is an important part of first impressions. Begin by shaking hands straight up and down. Speech makes a difference to the impression a person makes. Men who speak in a slow, deep voice seem in control. While it may not come naturally to change the tone of your voice, you should try to speak slowly and clearly in the first few moments of the interview.

Arriving on time

Early arrival is part of the interview preparation. Check your appearance. Read your letter of invitation to attend and remember any names on it.

If the interview is going to be one where you meet other interviewees, there are even more reasons to arrive early. Weigh up the other candidates. Make an effort to get on with them so that you appear to fit in. However, you may meet an interviewee who is obviously not the sort of person who will get the job. Perhaps he is too outspoken, or badly dressed. Keep well away from him! If you associate with him, you may be tarred with the same brush. His behaviour could damage your chances of getting the job.

Creating a good first impression

The following behaviour creates a good impression. You are quietly confident, and enter with a smile. Walk in with an open manner, using open gestures. This means not clenching your fists, teeth, etc. or crossing your arms or legs (though it is acceptable for women to cross their legs). The most open gesture possible is facing the interviewer, with your arms down and the palms of your hands facing forward. You must always keep your hands out of your pockets. Keep your head up and both hands visible. Face the interviewer all the time. Avoid scratching your head, nose or anything else! Mannerisms can give away nervousness. Most people are nervous at interviews, but do your best to hide it. Successful candidates behave confidently despite their nervousness.

The interviewer may make comments that are intended to put you at ease. In reality, he may be just as anxious himself, and it is important for you to put him at ease too.

Shake hands straight up and down. Use a slow, deep voice. Smile, and look the interviewer in the eye for a short time. Too short a time and you will be considered timid; too long and you will be judged overfamiliar. Above all, convey a sense of confidence and easiness. Easiness is a kind of neutral friendliness that makes the interviewer feel comfortable. At this stage, you must not be too friendly. If things go well, you will naturally increase your level of friendliness as the interview progresses. If things seem to go badly, bear in mind that your impression might be wrong. Therefore, continue to become more friendly as the interview progresses. However, avoid becoming too familiar.

Sit only when invited, and in the chair that is offered. If placed opposite a bright window or in an uncomfortable position, do not worry. This will be an oversight. It is not an interview ploy. Simply point out the problem and the interviewer will rearrange the seating.

You will also have to be flexible and appropriate. Having done your preparation, you have freed up time in which to use your wits.

INTERVIEW CHECK LIST

To help on the day of the interview, which may be hectic, use a check list. Here is an example:

Polish shoes
Bath
Clean teeth
Trim fingernails
Straighten tie
Copies of CV and other documents
Interview invitation
Check interview time and date
Copies of home and company phone numbers for emergency
Money, comb and handkerchief
Road map
Packed lunch and drink
Watch
Cassette tapes for car radio

Chapter 12

Practice

Some people use interviews for practice. This is a bad plan, for two reasons. First, the rejection letter that is bound to follow is a psychological setback. You will begin to doubt your own worth and ability and enter a cycle of defeat. Second, the wasted job chance may be the best one that you get.

Suppose you do not really want the advertised vacancy. Big companies often have several vacancies they might consider you for. Being prepared and flexible might mean the chance of one of those jobs. You make an impression that the interviewer will remember for the future. Maybe another opportunity will arise in the same company at a later date. It would be good to leave an impression that keeps the door open to future opportunities.

It is unusual to be offered a job when only attending the interview for practice. Lack of preparation normally creates the impression of lack of interest, and the interviewer's decision is a subjective generalisation: this candidate is unsuitable for work.

There are different ways to practise.

- alone, in writing
- alone, speaking aloud, on audio or video tape
- in a mock interview with someone pretending to interview you, on audio or video tape
- as a full dress rehearsal, if possible on video

It is natural to progress through these different stages. The first suggestion builds a solid foundation for the remaining stages, and so deserves the lion's share of the available time and effort.

Practising alone, in writing

Chapter 13 deals with some common interview questions and how to answer them. You should also have prepared a list of your main achievements and decided which ones to emphasise at the forthcoming job interview.

Choose some questions that you think might be asked. Write down your answers. Next, practise writing down the replies without referring to previous notes.

You need to be able to recall your key selling points instantly on demand. You will be surprised how useful it is if you can recite short phrases at the interview without having to think too hard.

Include a written reply to the worst question that might be asked. Check that the reply fits in with your key selling points and that it will not lead to negative probing.

Rehearse your career history. How can you modify it to answer the various possible opening questions? Repeatedly writing down your replies, without referring to any previous notes, is tedious but worthwhile. Each time, compare your replies with your previous ones. Note any omissions. As a guide, expect to spend about a third to half the available time practising your introductory career history. It has to be perfect.

When possible, practise ahead of receiving an invitation to attend an interview. Pick a job and practise as if you had been invited to an interview for it. Different jobs should require only minor changes.

Practising alone, speaking aloud

One way to rehearse answers is to list what you think are the ten interview questions most likely to come up. Include a question about your career history, and the question that you are most afraid of. Prepare written replies first.

The best way to begin practising is in private, where no one can overhear or criticise. It is a good idea to progress to tape-recording the answers. Listen carefully to yourself. Your answers should sound fluent and confident.

Work on the answers so that they come across as spontaneous, enthusiastic and energetic. Include words such as *enjoyed*, *interesting* and *exciting*. Anticipate the probing questions that will follow, and think about what to say.

Look at the recording as a whole:

- Did the key points come over?
- Were the key points put across clearly and one at a time?
- Did each reply sound positive the whole of the time?
- Did any self-deprecation creep in?
- Did you use the words *only*, *small* or *minor* when talking about your achievements?

Tape-recording questions and answers has an additional benefit: on the journey to the interview you can play back the tape on the car cassette player. However, you must remember that building self-esteem is also an important part of the job search. On the day, a positive frame of mind is essential.

When the prepared questions and answers are perfected and sound convincing, ask someone else to read out the questions from a list that you have prepared. This mock interview will build confidence each time it is repeated.

The mock interview

The people affected by your job, by whether you have a job and how well it pays, are unable to attend the interview with you. Parents, or when you are married, your spouse would like to do something to help. The mock interview is their chance to contribute. However, these people, however well-intentioned, should remember that criticism is damaging. The job-seeker is practising in order to raise his self-confidence, not to have it destroyed.

You need a room containing a table and two chairs. Some

interviews are held across the table, and others with both the interviewer and the candidate on the same side of the table. Prepare for an across-the-table interview, where body language is less important.

Begin the mock interview by entering the room, smiling confidently. The interviewer forms an impression within the first ten seconds, so this is a crucial time to rehearse. You should hold yourself upright, smile and make good eye contact. Shake hands firmly and straight up and down. Sit only when invited to.

The stand-in interviewer should ask questions only from the list that the candidate has prepared, and should resist asking questions of his own. It is best if the stand-in does not attempt to think of his own questions because they are unlikely to be totally relevant. Unlikely questions might derail the plan to lead the real interviewer to ask positive questions.

Record the interview on audio at least, and on video if possible. It is important to discuss how the interview went. At this stage, new questions or modifications to replies can be suggested. Repeat the mock interview until no further improvements can be made.

What was your body language like? Your posture needs to be strong, open and confident. You can achieve this by sitting with your knees slightly apart, keeping your hands relaxed and open. Sitting very slightly forward will project energy and interest. Avoid fidgeting, sitting on your hands or steepling your fingers. All these mannerisms will annoy the interviewer, even if it is only subconsciously. Above all, never put both hands behind your head. That is a sign of overconfidence and is too familiar for an interview. Most people need to give some thought to body language, as the correct behaviour rarely comes naturally.

If at first you cannot manage without, it is acceptable to read from a prepared manuscript of replies. That is preferable to learning incorrect answers during the mock interview. Once the replies are right, concentrate on the body language to support them.

The full dress rehearsal

You want to feel comfortable dressed in the clothes you will wear at the interview. It helps to wear them for a dress rehearsal. Naturally, you want to try on your best suit and all the accoutrements well ahead of the day of the interview. For a full dress rehearsal you also need a haircut and manicure. Avoid a last-minute rush to do these things. It spoils composure, and you always forget something. As a guideline, aim to do a complete dress rehearsal one week ahead of the interview. Taken seriously, a dress rehearsal builds confidence and is really worthwhile.

Polish your interview shoes and select the right tie. Ties are important because the male interview uniform is so rigid. A bright patterned tie portrays aggression, and for many jobs a go-getting image is the right one.

You should have a reserve outfit ready just in case of mishaps. Everything must be neatly laundered and pressed, and it all takes time.

If possible, video the dress rehearsal. Play it back to see how you can improve for the real thing. Would you give this person the job? If not, why not? If so, why? What went well? Can you repeat it?

Chapter 13

Questions and Answers

For the sake of preparation, let us assume that there will be two interviews. One will be with the company personnel manager and the other with a line manager.

Question: How did your journey go? (either interviewer)
Answer: It went very well, thank you. I didn't have any delays and the map you provided was excellent.

Any similar reply will be satisfactory. The interviewer does not really want to know about your journey. He asks this question to allow you time to settle in. You must reply positively by saying that things went well. Do not start complaining about the weather or the traffic. Both you and the interviewer probably feel a little nervous. To reassure the interviewer, and to put him at ease, you need to respond reassuringly, to build up a positive atmosphere in which the serious questioning may begin.

Interviewer's introductory statement (personnel manager)

Quite often the interview begins with a statement about the company, its history, and the particular job vacancy. It is Personnel's function to provide this kind of background information and to help with administrative duties like travelling expenses.

The personnel manager will try to weigh you up by watching your reactions to what is said. These are as important as your verbal answers to questions.

The personnel manager will report his impression to the line manager and anyone else involved in the recruitment decision.

The personnel manager's opinion may get you the job, or, alone, can prevent you from getting it.

You should use body language to display an interest in the vacancy. You must treat the personnel manager courteously, listening attentively to what he says, nodding and saying 'Yes' at intervals to show that you understand. You must avoid fidgeting, which is rude because it shows a lack of interest. You will also show interest by giving the interviewer intermittent eye contact.

Question: What do you already know about this company? (either interviewer)
Answer: I have heard a lot about the company and know that it is expanding fast and has factories in Europe and Japan.

If asked what you already know, you should reply that you know a lot, and give an example. It does not matter if that is all you know, because it is the interviewer's job to tell you about the company, not vice versa. The interviewer will normally take things up and explain in detail about the set-up. You must look interested when the interviewer talks about the company.

Even a short statement such as the above reply requires preparation. It is hard to make up one or two coherent points on the spot. If you have prepared, it shows. The interviewer will be pleased. If you have not prepared and cannot say something about the company, the interviewer will be unimpressed.

You need to sound enthusiastic in a way that invites the interviewer to tell you more. Normally, an interviewer asks this question to signal that he is about to describe the company. The question normally arises early in the interview, and if it is handled badly your reply can spoil the rest of the proceedings. If you say that you do not know anything about the company, or use words like 'only' or 'not very much', you will create a bad impression.

In reply to this initial question about what you know, it is not a good idea to volunteer technical information. However, if you go armed with one or two facts about profits and turnover, you are well prepared to handle any probing questions such as the next one.

Question: What else do you know about the company? (either interviewer)
Answer: Well, I know a lot, but I'm not sure where to begin. Can you tell me why you are asking?

If you are unsure about why the interviewer has asked this question, say so, and invite him to clear up the confusion. He might ask what you have found out about the company before attending the interview. If you can then show that you know a few salient facts, he will be impressed.

Question: What do you know about the job? (personnel manager)
Answer: I understand what the job is. [Say what it is.] I am used to doing this sort of work. It is what I did in my holiday job/previous job, and I'm excited about the possibility of doing it here. I think I could do a good job.

Explain the relevance of your experience, qualifications and training. Tell the interviewer that you can do the job and let him know that you want the job.

Let us look at why the personnel manager might ask this question. He may want to find out if you are really interested in the job. Someone who is interested in the job will surely know what it is. The personnel manager also wants reassuring that you yourself are confident that you can do the job.

Question: What do you know about the job? (line manager)
Answer: I understand what the job is, and I'm sure I can do it. However, I would be interested to know more.

If the line manager asks this question, he probably wants to make sure that you really do understand what the job is, so that he can be sure you still want the job, and you remain confident that you can do it.

The line manager will normally go on to explain the job in detail. As he does so, you should nod in agreement and say 'Yes' from time to time. In other words, you must be an active, interested listener. You should pick out things from the job description that you have done before and mention your experience if possible. You should link your own talk about your career history and achievements to the new information provided by the line manager.

It is rude to interrupt if the interviewer goes on a bit. Remember, it is the interviewer who controls the interview and not the candidate. Unfortunately, managers do tend to ramble on about the job. This is a problem when it leaves insufficient time for the candidate to talk about his key selling points. There are two possibilities to consider when this happens. Either the manager is satisfied that the candidate could do the job and is now trying to persuade him to take it. Or, the manager is unable to think of any more questions and is stalling. The first possibility is the more likely if it happens at the end of the interview. In this case the candidate should leave well alone. However, if it happens at the beginning of the interview, the candidate should try to suggest questions to the interviewer.

You can find out if something an interviewer says is meant as a question by saying: 'Yes, I had a similar experience. Would you like me to tell you about it?' The interviewer can then ask about that if he wants to.

The problem of the rambling interviewer is particularly acute if the candidate is unaware of how long the interview will last and thus does not know how much time remains for him to get over his key selling points.

Suppose an interviewer has spent five to ten minutes talking about the job without asking any questions. You must tell the interviewer about your strengths and selling points to have a chance of getting the job. A description of your career history takes less than two minutes but it sets the agenda for the remainder of the interview. Once the interviewer has finished speaking, you can make the following suggestion: 'I am very interested to hear about the job, and it sounds exactly what I want. Would you like me to tell you how it fits in with my own experience?'

If that is too much, then 'Fine, can I tell you a bit about myself now, please?' will do the trick just as well.

Following your description of your career, if the interviewer still does not ask any questions, you can continue to press home each key point by saying: 'You said [something the interviewer mentioned] and I had a similar experience at company X. Would you like me to tell you about it?'

You should limit yourself to two minutes' talking before you give the interviewer the chance to take control of the interview again.

You have to get your key selling points over, no matter how inept the interviewer is. But bear in mind that someone who cannot interview probably has other strengths, so do not judge the interviewer too harshly. One possible reason for the line manager's inadequate preparation is that he has been too busy getting on with the job. Maybe that is the sort of person it would be good to work with.

Question: How did you enjoy working at company X? (line manager)
Answer: I enjoyed it very much. One of the most exciting jobs I did was [best achievement].

This open question gives you the opportunity to sell yourself. The interviewer is not genuinely interested in whether a candidate enjoyed working at company X or not, but he does want to know something about the things the candidate did there. You must use the question either to outline your career history or to explain one of your key selling points or strengths. The safest option is to choose a single main achievement and talk about it for between one and two minutes. Trying to explain too much at once is not effective. Saying too little is to miss a great opportunity.

Incidentally, you must say that you really enjoyed your work, or you risk entering a negative spiral of questioning about why not! Interviewers will think that a candidate who has not enjoyed a previous job would not enjoy a future one either.

The answer to a question about how you enjoyed a previous job must supply some information about what you have achieved. It must also describe how you feel about your achievements.

Question: Why did you leave your last job? *or* Why do you want to leave your current job? (either interviewer)
Answer: 'I wanted more money' (*or* 'I wanted better prospects'; *or* 'I wanted to widen my experience'; *or* 'I was interested in [whatever you did next] and then I got the chance to do it).

You should always phrase your reasons for moving in a positive way, and think ahead to avoid a series of negative questions. For example, it would be a mistake to say: 'I was not getting enough responsibility', or even 'I wanted more responsibility'. These replies might make the interviewer feel that you are not the sort of person who can be given responsibility. That is all right if you have had a more responsible job since, otherwise it may be better to choose a different reason.

If asked why you are leaving your current job, a good reply is to claim: 'I am happy at [my present employer] but also ambitious. This job will provide me with greater challenge and opportunity.'

Question: What did you get out of your job at company X? (either interviewer)
Answer: I gained a lot of useful experience and learned a great deal. One of my most interesting jobs was to [a main achievement and key selling point].

You have to be positive and sound enthusiastic. Your experience is what you are selling to the interviewer. This question is an open question that you should use constructively. The answer should last between one and two minutes and get over one of your key selling points.

Question: What was your most worthwhile achievement at company X? (line manager)

Answer: I completed several memorable achievements. I think the one that I would pick out as the most worthwhile was [an achievement] because it [solved a problem/was a challenge/made a lot of money/improved quality, etc.].

You should then go on to describe what you did. This question is an open question inviting you to tell the interviewer about a main achievement. Remember to use it in support of a key selling point. For example, if you led a team of people to complete a task it could be used to show organisational skills. Alternatively an achievement might prove problem-solving, leadership or thinking skills. You must decide which skills are required for the job and link your experience to them.

Question: Tell me about a job you did that went terribly wrong or turned out badly. (either interviewer)

Answer: None of my jobs ever went terribly wrong.

If pressed to give an example, it must be something unimportant and that would be unlikely to happen again. You can emphasise that you learned from the experience and now always do things differently. An example could be that you borrowed a pool car from work to go on an important visit the following day, and that the next morning the car would not start. After that, you were careful never to park a pool car so that it was impossible to get your own car out.

Question: Which job at company X did you enjoy the most? (*or* Tell me about a job you enjoyed a lot.) (either interviewer)

Answer: I enjoyed doing [whatever] because it gave me a feeling of team membership. I had particular responsibility for [something], and because it went well I felt I had made a worthwhile contribution. When the team was successful, I felt it was worth all of the effort that I had made to overcome the problems.

This is an easy question. Most people can think of something they enjoyed a lot. The important thing is to use the opportunity to get over one of your key selling points. In the above answer, the idea is to claim that you can work in a team by describing how you worked as a team member in the past. You enjoyed being a part of the team, and understood what your contribution to the team effort was.

Question: Which job at company X did you enjoy the least? (either interviewer)
Answer: I cannot remember any jobs that I did not enjoy at all. However, if I had to pick the job I enjoyed the least, it would be doing a traffic survey outside the factory. I felt that it was an unwelcome distraction and would rather that someone else had done it.

This is dangerous territory. It could lead to a series of negative probing questions. Remember that if things went wrong it is hard to convince people that it was not your fault. In the above reply, it would be difficult to explain why you were picked for an unpopular job. You might be ready to save the situation, if the need arises, by relating how you got local schoolchildren involved in the exercise. That would turn the negative situation of an unpopular job into the positive achievement of liaising outside the company to organise something useful.

Question: Why did you take the job at company X? (either interviewer)
Answer: The job was what I had always wanted to do. It gave me the opportunity to learn new skills, and the experience I gained there was invaluable to me. I feel that I made a real contribution, particularly by doing [something that you hope to be asked more about], but now is the time to move on.

Question: How does your career so far [or your degree course] match up to your expectations? (either interviewer)
Answer: Generally, I think it is about what I expected. It is

116

very difficult to know what to anticipate when beginning a career. I have enjoyed it very much and I'm very pleased with the experience I have gained. I now look forward to spending a period in [whatever the vacancy is], and I'm enthusiastic about the future.

Question: Tell me about your current job. (line manager)

This is an open invitation to describe your career history. Replies should last for between one and two minutes, and set the agenda for the remainder of the interview. Make sure that the tone of your reply is strongly positive. For example, an answer could begin: 'My present work at company X involves some particularly interesting and exciting jobs. I have a range of responsibilities that I enjoy, including [something you would like to be asked about].'

Question: How do you get on with your current boss? (either interviewer)
Answer: I like him very much. He is easy to get on with.

The interviewer wants clues about how you will get on with your potential new manager, so be positive. Keep your reply short to be believable.

Question: What has been your most serious disagreement with your boss? (either interviewer)
Answer: I cannot remember ever disagreeing with my boss.

Question: What is the most important strength that you bring to this job? (line manager)
Answer: I believe that I'm particularly good at solving problems methodically, which is something that I enjoy. An example of a recent problem that I solved was [an achievement you hope to be asked about].

This can be a frightening question if you are not prepared for it. The question is quite open, allowing virtually any reply. It is a good idea to link the strength to the job on offer, and to support the claim with a work example.

Question: Why did you choose the particular career that you have embarked on? (either interviewer)
Answer: I always enjoyed [the relevant subject] at school, and that made me think of it as a career. I found out more by reading about it and asking the people I met.

Question: What do you think you will be doing in five years' time? (either interviewer)
Answer: I feel I can make a real impact in this vacancy, and would like to do this sort of work for a while. I see myself building up a record of achievement in this or similar work. In the long term, I have got in mind that eventually I would like to get into line management [or whatever else you want to do]. Of course that will depend on how things go and the kind of opportunities that arise.

Interviewers often ask this question. However, the value of it is limited since no one can look into the future. You can, however, use the question to show that you are ambitious, if you think that is what the interviewer wants. It is important to show a flexible response, because you do not know what the interviewer is thinking.

Question: Have you any questions? (either interviewer, asked towards the end of the interview)
Answer: Who would be my new boss if I were to be offered the job?

When asked if you have any questions, the easy option is to say 'No.' Candidates are often afraid of asking silly questions that might spoil their chance of being offered the job. However, by saying nothing, you miss the opportunity to make a parting impression. This parting impression has to be one of interest. With a question, you imply that you are still interested in the job and would take it if offered.

118

Perhaps you consider that asking about your new boss is silly. Maybe you think the interviewer will suspect that you have doubts about whether you will get on together. It is an inappropriate question if the interviewer has already told you that he would be your new boss. If this is the case, you may still confirm your interest in the job by saying: 'I have not got any questions, but I would like to take this opportunity to confirm that I am still interested in the job. Thank you for taking the time to interview me.'

A question about who would be your new boss is a good idea because he will have a great influence on your future and it will be important that you get on with him. Should you already know who your boss would be, you can ask a different question, such as: 'Can you tell me a bit more about my prospective new boss?' Alternatively, if the interviewer does not know who your new boss would be you could ask about the *sort* of person he might be: his background and experience, for example.

If you do not think you can get on with the boss, do not take the job.

There may be other questions you would like to know the answers to. For example, what will the salary be? What are the pension, health-care and holiday arrangements? However, if the interviewer did not explain these things himself, it is probably wise just to wait and see.

Chapter 14

Interview Surprises

Interviews are rarely without their surprises. Here are two ways to limit the damage:

- Find out as much as possible before the interview.
- Prepare for the expected parts. Rehearse a description of your career history to deliver at the start of the interview. Prepare the answers to frequent questions. This frees up thinking time at the interview to cope with the things that are genuinely unforeseeable.

Candidates who adopt a flexible attitude at the interview will be best placed to take advantage of the unexpected. An interview surprise can become an opportunity. The following are some common interview surprises.

THE PANEL INTERVIEW

A panel interview is when more than one person interviews the candidate simultaneously. Panel interviews are more difficult than one-to-one interviews because it is harder to establish a rapport with two or more interviewers. However, panel interviews with only two interviewers are much easier for the candidate than those with three or more. I shall describe them separately.

Panel interviews with two interviewers

When two interviewers share an interview, one or other, or both, might be inexperienced and need a second opinion. It is very sensible to interview in this way so that afterwards the interviewers can discuss their separate impressions of the candidate.

Another reason to have two interviewers is to expose the candidate to as many company people as possible in the shortest time. In a recruitment exercise, time is always at a premium. An interviewer sitting in the background, not asking questions, can observe the candidate's body language more easily. This is harder for the candidate, who needs to sell himself twice. If both interviewers ask questions from time to time, the candidate is more likely to settle down quickly. He should aim to act as if there is only one interviewer.

It is particularly important for the candidate to make sure that he knows why an interviewer has asked a question. If he is unsure then the other interviewer may be too. One technique is to repeat the question back to the interviewer. You must not get flustered. The way in which you handle this potentially difficult interview situation could get you the job. You should attempt to treat the two interviewers with equal courtesy and give some eye contact to each. Do not forget to describe your career history, and to follow it up with your key selling points.

Incidentally, a spur-of-the-moment decision to invite a colleague to join in the interview is a sign that the interviewer is close to offering the candidate the job, but wants a second opinion. In these circumstances do not count on getting the job. This is as much a sign of the interviewer's indecision as it is of the candidate's suitability.

Panel interviews with more than two interviewers

A proper panel interview often involves four or five interviewers. Each has a different perspective. One may ask something for a reason that the others know nothing about. The other interviewers may therefore misinterpret the candidate's reply. It is hard for the candidate to do himself justice. Any series of probing questions is very confusing, and gives the candidate little chance to make a good impression.

121

Sometimes interviewers do not listen to the candidate's replies to other people's questions. They then go on to ask questions that, as far as the candidate is concerned, are out of context.

Sometimes interviewers ask questions to score points with the other members of the panel. The candidate does not know anything about it, and cannot understand what is going on.

Panel interviews can be handled best if the candidate is aware in advance that it is going to be a panel interview. He should enquire about this as early as possible and try to discover who will be on the panel and what their job functions are. This information might be available through the personnel department, and could be obtained over the telephone.

Whether or not a candidate expects a panel interview, he must be flexible enough to cope with one when it happens. His main concern must be to remain cool. He should remember to recite his career history early in the interview, and check that he has mentioned his key selling points towards the end.

In a panel interview:

- More of the decision-making has already been done. Therefore, a good CV is disproportionately important.
- There is less opportunity to outline your career history early in the interview, so make a special effort.
- When faced with probing questions, ask why the interviewer wants to know. This is for the benefit of the other interviewers too.
- Stick to predetermined selling points. Do not get bogged down with side issues.
- Answer the person who asked the question.
- Recognise that some interviewers may feel threatened by you, fearing that ultimately you will take their job. Such interviewers will try to put the others off you by asking difficult questions. If you recognise this to be the case, ask 'Why do you want to know?' It may be difficult for the questioner to explain. Other interviewers should recognise the situation and rescue you.

Panel interviews can be a no-win situation for the candidate. A possible strategy for coping with them is to have a good CV, to draw attention to your strengths during the interview, and get out quickly!

UNFAMILIAR SURROUNDINGS

This is a common interview surprise. Candidates need to arrive early and find out where the interview will be.

Normally, the interview will be in the interviewer's own office, in complete privacy and with no interruptions. The telephone should be redirected for the duration of the interview. However, unorganised interviewers sometimes take telephone calls and allow interruptions. This is unfair to the candidate, who then finds it difficult to concentrate on the interview. He may thus form a poor impression of the person who will be his manager. This in turn will influence his behaviour and spoil the interview.

Small organisations, or ones in rapid growth, might find it hard to accommodate an interview. The invitation to attend ought to warn candidates if this is the case. Conducting an interview in the canteen, or standing in a bus queue waiting to cross town, is not fair to the candidate. The lack of privacy inhibits interviewees more than it inhibits interviewers.

Coping with an unexpected venue is a challenge. Remember the importance of outlining your career history early in the interview. Remember that the key selling points need to be communicated clearly, one at a time. Do not be put off, no matter how offputting the circumstances become.

ANOTHER VACANCY

Big companies often have more than one vacancy at any time. If the interviewer starts talking about another vacancy it is tempting to show single-mindedness by saying that you are interested in the advertised job in particular. After all, convincing the interviewer of a genuine interest in the vacancy is an essential part of your job-search plan. You can demonstrate your flexibility, however, by expressing interest in the new vacancy and agreeing to being considered for it.

A different job would not be mentioned merely to see if you are genuinely interested specifically in the advertised job. That ploy would disrupt the interview.

The interviewer probably thinks you are not suitable for the advertised vacancy, or has seen a better candidate. However, he thinks that you could do a different job and so mentions the vacancy.

AGGRESSION

Interviewers sometimes behave aggressively, or abrasively, to see how well candidates stand up for themselves. Imagine that the job requires negotiation with unions. An interviewer might consider it appropriate to test your resilience by being abrasive. He asks personal questions to see if you object, which you should do. This unpleasant ploy can be countered by asking the interviewer why he or she wants to know, politely explaining that you cannot understand the relevance of the question.

Since the interviewer is completely in control of the interview, it is unfair for him to become aggressive. However, you must never be rude in return. A suggested approach is simply not to reply to the offending question. All you have to do instead is to answer a different, unasked question. That avoids confrontation.

If the interviewer raises his voice, you must remain quietly in control. He may pretend to become more agitated, in which case you must pretend to be unperturbed.

Candidates can be so upset by an aggressive interview that they decide not to work for a company that would use this tactic. In the short term there may be the chance of a job. However, in the longer term it is better to avoid a wrong career move. You might have to leave the company if you cannot get on with the other people who work there.

You should collect what information is available, including the position and influence of the interviewer. Do rude people do well in this company? Is this a way in which you could get on? Maybe it is an easy route upwards and onwards for some people. If you can succeed at abrasiveness, this is your kind of company.

UNEXPECTED GENDER OR COLOUR OF INTERVIEWER

Sometimes we build up an image in our minds of what another person might look like. At a job interview it is common for the only information about someone to be their name. Names give clues about sex, religion or ethnic background. These suppositions are sometimes wrong. When a mental image is shattered it is a disorienting surprise.

You need a flexible attitude. Think in advance about whether you would mind working for someone of the opposite sex or a different race. If these things are thought out beforehand, they are easier to cope with at the interview.

ACCEPT THE JOB OFFER, RIGHT NOW!

On occasion it comes as a surprise to be offered the job on the spot. Sometimes an interviewer might phone the candidate the same evening to make the offer. When asked whether they want the job or not, candidates need to know how to reply. If a candidate asks for time to consider, he may find the offer is withdrawn and made to someone else. Be prepared to reply if the need arises.

If offered the job, ask when it will be confirmed in writing. Do not cancel other job interviews and applications until the offer is confirmed in writing. Some employers will offer less money in the written confirmation. Some even withdraw the offer when they realise that you will not reach agreement on salary.

LUNCH WITH A COLLEAGUE

It is common for an interviewee to be asked to join a potential future colleague for lunch. Afterwards the interviewer will ask the future colleague for his impression of the candidate.

Normally, interviewers tell the candidate that the lunch is not a part of the interview. However, it is unavoidable that the person who accompanies the candidate to lunch will form an opinion of him. If the interviewers are unsure about the candidate, this opinion can tip the balance.

This lunch is supposed to be the candidate's opportunity to ask some questions off the record. However, it is wise to be cautious. Your future credibility is at stake. You should have a positive but polite manner, and should avoid giving away your feelings or opinions. If you say anything unusual, it is likely to be repeated. The art of being a good conversationalist is to be a good listener. You need to get the host to do most of the talking to create the best impression.

Remember that a future colleague will act out of self-interest. You might appear a threat to the colleague, who would then want to put you off joining the company. Alternatively, he might put the company off selecting you.

Interviewees should not reveal too much over lunch.

QUIZZES ON THE CANDIDATE'S PRESENT OR LATEST EMPLOYER

Candidates are expected to be knowledgeable about their latest employer. A lack of interest in your company's turnover and profit, for example, creates a poor impression.

INTELLIGENCE AND PERSONALITY TESTS

Tests for analytical thinking, conceptual thinking, numeracy, personality, etc. are described in Chapter 3. A good night's sleep is vital if a candidate is to perform well.

NO PARKING SPACES, OR LATE FINISHING

The candidate is expected to arrive on time no matter what the circumstances, and must be prepared to stay as long as it takes to complete the interview.

SIMILARITY TO A PREVIOUS OR PRESENT JOB

Sometimes a candidate is invited to interview because a similarity exists between his present job and the job vacancy. A candidate who does not know about this similarity will react badly when the interviewer mentions it.

Candidates need to check any product or technology similarities between companies so that they can make sensible comments at the interview. If they cannot, or if the interviewer discovers their ignorance, they will be unlikely to get the job.

ANOTHER INTERVIEW

If a candidate expects that an interview is the final stage in the selection procedure, and then finds that there will be another interview, he is bound to be disappointed. In this situation, he must bravely take things in his stride.

You should be able to agree to a date for a further interview if asked. A small diary containing important appointments comes in handy.

THE FACTORY VISIT

Where the employer runs a factory or plant, expect to go on a plant visit as part of the interview. These visits are often very enjoyable. You must not forget that you are at an interview, and you must not say anything in an unguarded moment during the plant visit.

You need to be especially aware of your impact on other employees. The person acting as guide on the factory visit will notice how current employees react to you. He wants to know that you could work well alongside them.

You should think before speaking, and abstain from passing judgement or opinions. This would be unwelcome. If asked for your opinion, you should give the middle-of-the-road answer.

GROUP EXERCISES

Group exercises are a sophisticated method of seeing how candidates interact, and so how they might get on with people at work. A favourite exercise is for a group of four or five candidates to be told that they have been marooned – either in a desert or on the moon. They are given a list of the things available to them, and must list these things in order of importance, first on an individual basis and then as a group. Questions such as whether a compass would work on the moon arise, and each candidate has to argue his case. Candidates are examined to see whether they have an opinion, how well they put it across, and if they can influence the others.

The best way to behave is in a quietly confident manner. You should express a point of view only when you know that you are right. Repeat what you say if challenged, without raising your voice or clenching your teeth or fists. Never repeat anything more than twice, and be prepared to accept other people's points of view.

The extent to which a candidate can influence the others and get his way depends on the rest of the group. If one candidate behaves particularly aggressively and dominantly, this candidate will be eliminated. Other candidates should avoid getting involved in any heated discussions or arguments with him.

The interviewers may notice your body language. Maintain open gestures and neutral expressions so that you appear assertive. Finally, you must be prepared to go with the group even if the group is wrong. Remember that the art of leadership is to watch which way people are going and then run to the front and shout 'Follow me!'

In these group exercises, it is tempting to adopt a position and then defend it. The temptation is even greater when the group is given a technical problem to which you think you have the answer. Remember that the game is to fit in with the others and get along with the group. Actually solving the problem is not as important.

THE EVENING MEAL

Big companies often use an evening event to expose candidates to as many company people as possible. The interviewers have a group discussion afterwards in which they share impressions of each candidate. It is important for the candidate not to get ruled out by behaving badly at the evening event.

Candidates are always told that the evening meal is not a part of the selection procedure. Realistically it must be, because the interviewers are powerless to ignore what goes on at it. The evening meal is often the first time that the interviewer sees the candidate, and it is thus when their crucial first impression is formed.

What to wear is a dilemma, though it is actually not that important. I recommend that you should be tidy, but don't wear your interview suit. You need to have a fresh outfit on, to make a fresh impression, at the interview the next day. For men, a sports jacket and tie, or a not too flashy second suit, are appropriate. At the other extreme, some candidates will wear a pullover and cord trousers.

Unless it is against their religion, candidates are expected to drink alcohol. The interviewers and company employees will drink, because for them this is a relaxing social event. The best advice for candidates is that they should have a drink at the beginning of the evening, and then stop. You need a clear head to create a deliberate impression.

Interviewers will be highly sensitive to how candidates get on with one another and the company employees, who are their potential future colleagues. It is important for candidates to share the values and standards of the existing employees.

It is not uncommon for one candidate to have a particularly outgoing personality, which will most likely be considered unsuitable or excessive. This candidate will be rejected. The trick as far as the other candidates are concerned is not to be rejected along with them. If you see someone who is obviously not the sort of person the company will want to employ, keep well away from them. Try not to sit next to them, and do not become engaged in lengthy conversation with them at any time.

Final-year undergraduates and new graduates may find the evening meal particularly arduous as they probably have no previous experience of eating out on business. I would advise them to be restrained and polite, but to chat easily with their hosts and one another. The event must not be an ordeal for the hosts. Avoid the temptation to subject them to a barrage of questions about the job. Leave that to someone else.

SALARY

Normally the exact salary is only mentioned in a firm written offer. The offer is then either accepted or declined. It is unusual for an improved offer to be made, but it does happen.

If offered a low salary for a job that you would like, it is worth mentioning your reason for rejecting the offer. You can always hope for, but not expect, an increased offer.

The personnel manager sometimes asks the candidate what salary he expects in order to find out if it is compatible with the company's probable offer. Candidates find it hard to say how much they expect. The rule is to be sure that the company want you before you ask a price. A company will pay over the odds for someone they really want. A candidate with several years' experience will be in a stronger negotiating position than a new graduate.

Do not settle for a low starting salary, because the starting salary forms the basis from which future rises or promotions are made. Candidates who accept a lower salary than they are content with are likely to want to move on again soon, and face the same problems again. When job-hunting next time, salary negotiations will be based on this initial low salary.

Salary is not the only consideration. If a job offers valuable experience that will allow a higher salary to be obtained later, that is a matter for individuals to weigh up. A few professions offer a very low initial salary, or years of study and training, before you start to earn really good money. Reputable schemes are worthwhile. Unfortunately, there are many examples of training schemes with no prospect of future reward. They offer low-paid jobs as an alternative to unemployment, a compromise that is only satisfactory for a short time.

Further Reading

Charles Margerison and Dick McCann, *Team Management, Practical New Approaches*. Management Books 2000 Ltd., Didcot, 1995.

The following are available at university careers offices:

Graduate Opportunities (GO). A Newpoint Publication, Hobsons Publishing plc. Also at web site http://www.get.co.uk.

Prospects Finalist and *Prospects Postgrad*. Published in six issues from November to June by the Higher Education Careers Services Unit, CSU Ltd., Manchester. Also at web site http://www.prospects.csu.man.ac.uk.

AGCAS (Association of Graduate Careers Advisory Services) Careers Information Booklets. CSU (Publications) Ltd., Armstrong House, Oxford Road, Manchester M1 7ED. Occupational Series subjects include: Education; Commerce; Financial and Legal; Manufacturing and Processing; Science; Engineering and Technology.

Ivanhoe Careers Guides (with details of key employers). Cambridge Market Intelligence Ltd., London House, Parkgate Road, London SW11 4NQ. Examples include:

The Ivanhoe Guide to Chartered Accountants, 1997
The Ivanhoe Guide to the Engineering Profession, 1997
The Ivanhoe Guide to Management Consultants, 1997
The Ivanhoe Guide to the Legal Profession, 1997
The Ivanhoe Guide to Information Systems, 1997
The Ivanhoe Guide to Marketing and Sales, 1997

The GTI Careers Journals. GTI, 6 Hithercroft Court, Lupton Road, Wallingford, Oxon OX10 9BT. Also at web site http://www.gti.co.uk. Subject examples include: City and Finance; Civil and Structural Engineering; Engineering; Law; Quantity Surveying; Water and Environment.

Other References

Dorothy Stewart, *Handbook of Management Skills*, a Gower Handbook, 1994.

Alan Pease, *Body Language: How to Read Others' Thoughts by their Gestures*, Sheldon Press, 1990.

David Hind, *Transferable Personal Skills*, Business Education Publishers, 1994.

Index

Accept the job, now 125
Accounts 12, 92
Achievements 32, 34, 40,
    44–47, 86, 87, 89, 115
Advertisements 12, 62–66
    agency 63
    calendar 64–65
    reading 87
Agency:
    advertisements 63
    outplacement 38, 70
    recruitment 40, 63–64,
        67, 70–71
Aggression 23–24, 124–125
Ambition 118
Annual reports, company 13
Another:
    interview 127
    vacancy 123–124
Application:
    forms 24, 55–61,
        76, 81–82
    speculative 67–73
Assertiveness 23–24, 29

Body language 17, 23, 102,
    107, 121, 128
Boss 13, 20, 33, 37, 56
    arguments with 88
    new 37, 118–119

reference from 61
    relationship 117
Brochures, company
    12, 76–77

CV 43–54
    example 49–53
    layout 46–47
    length 48
    memorising 87
    preparation 8, 38–39,
        44–46
    style 47–48
Career:
    fairs 74, 77
    history, spoken 95–97,
        112, 117
    history, written 44
    office 55, 67, 74, 76
Casualness 30
Check list:
    application forms 61
    interview 103
Choice, of job 8, 33–37
    of achievements
        87
Commitment to the
    job 20–21
Communication skills
    24–25

Company, big or small
33–35
research 92
Concern:
for efficiency 19
for impact 22–23
for standards 18
Confidence, self 21, 32
Contacts 69
Cover letter 9, 11, 62
example 54
Criticising previous
employer 17
Customer focus 13

Deliberate pause 16
Diagrams 24
Dress 17, 23, 99–101
for evening meal 129
rehearsal 108

Employer:
choice of 33–35, 37
current 126
Esteem, self- 26, 29,
30–32, 99
Evaluating information 22

Factory visit 127–128
Familiarity, over- 17
Family 37, 106
Flexibility 102, 122–123

Gender, unexpected 125
Graduate Opportunities
(*GO*) 65–66
Grooming 99
Group exercise 128

Hobbies 59, 80
Holiday job 47, 60, 78, 80

Impact:
concern for 22–23
opening 107
Impressions, first 101–102,
107
Initiative 59–60, 80
Instability 29
Intelligence 21, 30
tests 21, 30, 126
Internet 65–66, 76
Interview 8–9, 39–40
another 127
mistakes 12, 25, 57
mock 39, 106–107
panel 120–123
preparation 85–103
questions 33, 89–91,
109–119
self-esteem at 30
technique 39–40
uniform 99
Introductory statement 109

Job offer 130–131

Layout of CV 46–47
Length of CV 48
Letter, examples:
cover for CV 54
speculative application
72–73
Lunch with a colleague 126

Market research 11
Meal 129–130

Memorise:
  achievements 86
  CV 87
Message, your 12, 25, 57
Milk round 55, 66, 74–82
  timetable 74–76
Mistakes, interview
  12, 25, 57
Moving on 36–37

Nervousness 102, 109
Newspaper, advertisement
  calendar 64–65
Numbers game 8–9, 81

Offer 15
  job 130–131
Opportunity 15
Outplacement agency 38, 70
Overfamiliarity 17

Panel interview 120–123
Parking 127
Pension 14, 34–35, 119
Personality 26–32
  relating to job 27–28
  sorts 26–27
  tests 28, 126
Personnel
  function 14, 109
  manager's questions
    109–119
Plan 5–17
Positive reflection 16
Practise, interview 104–108
Preparation 7
  answers to questions 97,
    109–119

interview 85–103
  travel 98
Product, your 10
Professional help 38–40
  to avoid 40
Prospects Finalist 66
Prospects vs salary 36
Put-downs, avoid 32

Qualifications 47
Questions:
  application form 56–60
  interview 33, 89–91,
    109–119
  preparation 97–98
  telephone 12

Reading the advert 87
Recession 10, 37
Recruitment agency 40,
  63–64, 67, 70–71
Redundancy 30–31,
  34, 37, 46
References 31, 60–61
Reflection 16
Rejection 16, 33, 63
Research:
  company 11, 92
  market 11–13
  telephone 12, 68, 92, 122
Responsibility 58, 59
Review 16

Salary 36, 70, 119, 125,
  130–131
Sales jobs 63
Second interview 9
Selection criteria 14–15

Self confidence 21, 32
Self esteem 26, 29, 30–32
  building 99
  cycle 31
  low 31
Shotgun 9
Show off knowledge 93
Similarity to a previous
  job 127
Skills, reviewing 18–25
Specialisation 35
Speculative approaches
  67–73
  letters 67, 72, 73
Staged process 7–10
Strengths 10–11, 16, 33, 47,
  60, 91, 96
  most important 117
Style of CV 47–48
Subjective decisions 6, 14,
  30, 87, 96, 104
Surprises 30
  interview 120–131
Surroundings, unfamiliar 123

Talking too much 16
Teamwork 6, 22, 26,
  59–60, 87

Telephone:
  offer 125
  research 12, 68, 92, 122
  screening 64
Tests:
  intelligence 21, 30, 126
  personality 28, 126
Thinking skills 21
Time to move on 36
Timetable, for milk
  round 74–76
Transferable skills 18–25
Travel arrangements
  98–99, 127

Understanding others 22
Unexpected gender or
  colour 125
Unfamiliar surroundings 123

Vacancy, another 123
Voice 100, 101

Weaknesses 11, 16, 39
Work experience 78, 79